Modern

HYPNOSIS :

Theory and Practice

Masud Ansari, Ph. D.

Mas-Press
P.O. Box 57374
Washington, D.C. 20037

Second edition 1991

LIBRARY OF CONGRESS CATALOGING
IN PUBLICATION DATA

Library of Congress Catalog Card No. 81-69861
Ansari, Masud
Modern Hypnosis
Washington, D. C.:   Ansari, Masud
8770   810914
ISBN   0-9607984-0-4

PRINTED IN THE UNITED STATES OF AMERICA

Mas-Press
P.O. Box 57374
Washington, D.C. 20037

*Dedicated to those authors
referred to in this study,
to whom I am
forever indebted.*

PREFACE

Our forefathers could never have foreseen the stupendous development of science and technology that modern man takes for granted. Yet, even as we prepare to travel to other planets, we find ourselves to be psychologically less secure than our ancestors. As a result, technologically sophisticated modern man is compelled to take another journey, just as important as space travel, to find a cure for his psychological traumas and to secure inner peace. This journey is a sojourn into inner space, and its vehicle will most probably be hypnosis.

In this regard, S. J. Van Pelt, former president of the British Society of Medical Hypnotists and the author of a number of books on hypnosis, states: "Nobody, no matter how fanatically opposed to hypnotism, can deny that hypnosis is the most powerful and effective method of controlling the mind, and through the mind, the whole body." And according to Arthur Ellen: "Eighty per cent of the patients in our huge hospitals do not belong there, and could be helped by experts in hypnosis . . . Hypnosis is far more effective than psychoanalysis or psychotherapy."

These statements are particularly significant when we consider self-hypnosis. With the help of self-hypnosis, everyone can become his own healer, cure his psychological shortcomings, alter his attitudes, and modify his behavior.

These inspirations caused me to assign a chapter on "hypnosis," in one of my books on psychology (Frontiers in Psychology). Thereafter, my residence in Calcutta, India and Japan provided me a suitable opportunity to obtain a new insight into experimental hypnosis., particularly with an oriental hue. Since 1975, I have been living in England and the United States and have been privileged to further widen the scope of my knowledge of hypnosis by a plethora of research that had already been done by previous authors, mainly Arons, Barber, Cooke, Erickson, Fromm, Gindes, Hartland, Hilgard, Hull, Krasner, Kroger, LeCron, Marcuse, Sparks, Spiegel, Udolf, Van Pelt, Van Vogt, Weitzenhoffer, Wolberg, and others. With regard to experimental hypnosis I have been very much impressed by the mastery of Dr. A.M. Krasner, Chairman of the Board of the American Institute of Hypnotherapy.

This book, however, is the result of twenty years of study, research and practice of hypnosis. The contents of the book are so constituted as to be useful both for those who are investigating the theory and art of hypnosis, and for those who are interested in learning the practice of hypnosis.

I hope this effort will help those who are looking to take advantage of hypnosis as an effective modality for their self-improvement and self-development. And, finally, I hope that the book will contribute to the development of this science for the purpose of human well-being and that hypnosis will not be regarded as a tool to enhance power, influence, or prestige over others.

Masud Ansari, BA, MA, Ph.D., DCH, FCH
Washington, D.C. (1982).

REFERENCES

Ellen, A. and Jennings Dean, *The Intimate Casebook of a Hypnotist* (New York: New American Library, 1968), pp. 18-19.
Van Pelt, S. J., *Secrets of Hypnotism* (Hollywood, Ca.: Wilshire Book Co., 1958), p. 22.

CONTENTS

LIST OF ILLUSTRATIONS

CHAPTER ONE

THE HISTORY AND EVOLUTION OF HYPNOSIS

Hypnosis*, an art which has become an indispensable tool of medicine, psychotherapy and self-development, is as old as human history. From early times, there have been people who seemed to have the miraculous power of influencing the minds and bodies of other people. The powers of healing, practised by saints, priests, witch doctors, tribal leaders, and medicine men were thought of as miracles emanating from God.

The Egyptians, Greeks, Persians and Hindu fakirs used hypnosis thousands of years ago for therapeutic and religious purposes. There were healing places called *sleep temples* in ancient Greece and Egypt where patients were helped to relax by curative suggestions during their sleep. These suggestions were usually made by a combination of religious rituals and surgical procedures.

There are also references in both the Old and New Testa-

---

*According to Webster's Dictionary, *hypnosis* refers to the hypnotic state produced and *hypnotism* to the study of that state, but these terms are often used interchangeably. In this book *hypnosis* is used rather than *hypnotism*.

ments to evil spirits and their ability to take possession of people. In pre-Christian times, the Jews used professional exorcists.[1] These practices cannot be described as anything but what we know today as hypnosis.

Mesmer and the Genesis of Hypnosis

The modern history of hypnosis began with Friedrick (Franz) Anton Mesmer (1734-1815). In 1776, Mesmer, a Viennese physician, presented his thesis on "The Influence of the Stars and Planets on Curative Powers" to the Faculty of Medicine of the University of Vienna. In his thesis, Mesmer dealt with the notion that the stars and planets influence the human body. Influenced by Paracelsus'* theories; the exorcist-like techniques of Johan Gassner (1729-1779), a Catholic priest; and the ideas of Maximilian Hell (1720-1792), a Jesuit priest and astronomer, who healed sick people by applying steel plates to their body; Mesmer held that this influence occurred by means of a universal fluid (a kind of invisible magnetic fluid emanating from the stars and planets). Everybody possessed this impalpable fluid, but the sick had less than the healthy.

In Mesmer's view, ill-health originated from the unequal distribution of this fluid (magnetism) in the patient. Recovery could only be achieved by "magnetically" giving, removing, or redistributing the patient's animal magnetism using magnets. Mesmer later came to believe that the magnetic properties were within his own body and that magnets were unnecessary for the treatment of sick people. Because the curative

---

*Paracelsus (1493-1541) was a Swiss physician who believed that stars influenced human beings by their magnetic nature through invisible emanations.

effects of magnets could be obtained by making passes with bare hands over the afflicted parts of the patient's body, he also believed that animal magnetism in the same way could be transferred to an animal or inanimate object for curative purposes.

Earlier, Mesmer had made his patients silently sit in a group around an open tub or *baquet* from which magnetized metal bars protruded. Some would develop a kind of convulsive reaction usually accompanied by laughing or crying and sink into sleep. After several sessions they would be cured. Later, because he found "that magnetic properties were within his own body, he would simply touch the person, make passes with his hands, or touch water before his patients drank it."

Mesmer's reputation and success aroused the hostility and jealousy of the medical profession. Following an investigation he was forbidden by the medical society to practice in Vienna. Moving to Paris in 1778, however, he immediately achieved fame and great popularity.

As a result of the enmity of his colleagues and the concern created by Mesmer's activities, he asked the French Academy of Science to investigate his methods. A Commission of nine members was set up that included the American diplomat Benjamin Franklin, the French chemist, Antoine-Laurent Lavoisier, the physician, Guillotin (the inventor of the guillotine), and Antoine-Laurent de Jussieu, an outstanding botanist. The Commission did not take into account the therapeutic results obtained by means of magnetism. In 1784, it concluded that no evidence could be found for the physical existence of an animal magnetic fluid. The Commission did not deny the remarkable recoveries from illness, but related them to imagination and suggestion rather than magnetism. The Commission also pointed out that "mesmerism" was a definite menace to public morals because of the convulsions produced and the close physical contact between magnetizer and magnetized.

The report of the Commission put an end to any serious belief in magnetism and it was left to Mesmer's followers to develop his theory. Deeply discouraged and branded a quack, Mesmer left France in 1785. After traveling through Europe, he retired to a German village and later died in poverty and obscurity in Switzerland in 1815.

Puysegur and Artificial Somnambulism

The hypnotic state as it is known today, was discovered accidentally in 1784 by a retired French military man and follower of Mesmer, the Marquis de Puysegur (1781-1825). One day while he was applying Mesmer's magnetism to a 24 year-old shepherd, Victor Race, he observed a few hypnotic phenomena unknown to Mesmer. He noticed that the magnetized subject, instead of showing the usual "mesmeric convulsions" or unpleasant effects, fell into a peaceful sleep. In this state, the subject was able to open his eyes, talk in a slurred manner and act as if he were awake. Puysegur called this "artificial somnambulism." The magnetized subject could hear only what the magnetist said and was oblivious to others. And upon awakening the "magnetized" subject was not able to recall what had happened during the trance period.

These findings led Puysegur to the conclusion that the operator could control the thoughts and actions of the subject during the trance state, and that during the trance, the mind of the subject could remain alert, often even showing intelligence superior to their normal waking state.

Deleuze and Post-Hypnotic Suggestion

Another step forward towards the evolution of hypnotism was taken when a follower of Puysegur, Joseph Philippe Francois Deleuze (1753-1835), Librarian of the French Royal Botanical and Zoological Gardens, discovered that suggestions given to the patient during the hypnotic trance would be carried over into the waking state. This phenomenon is now called response to post-hypnotic suggestion. Both Puysegur and Deleuze, while they were fluidists, considered mesmerism a psychological phenomenon rather than a mechanical one as Mesmer did. In contrast to modern views, Puysegur and Deleuze thought hypnosis was produced by the magnetizer rather than by the subject.[2]

Faria and the Willingness of the Subject

In 1815, Jose Custodio de Faria (1755-1819), a wandering Portuguese priest, discovered that mesmerism was the product of the subject's characteristics and that the willingness and cooperation of the subject was a necessary condition for the successful production of animal magnetism, or what he called "Lucid Sleep." He believed that animal magnetism was not successful with a resistant subject.

Elliotson and the Dawn of Anaesthesia by Mesmerism

In 1837, John Elliotson (1791-1868), a professor of surgery at University College in London and inventor of the stethoscope, began mesmeric research using mesmerism at his hospital to perform painless surgery and treatment of nervous disorders. Soon this brought about difficulties. The prestigious British Medical Journal, *Lancet,* condemned him as a charlatan, and the council of the college forbade the application of mesmerism in University College Hospital, whereupon Elliotson resigned his post.

Elliotson continued to fight for mesmerism and in 1846, published the *Zoist,* a quarterly journal dealing with hypnosis in which numerous medical and painless surgeries observed by Elliotson and others during mesmeric trance were reported.

Esdaile and Anaesthesia by Mesmerism

In 1842 Dr. James Esdaile (1808-1859) a Scottish surgeon in charge of a special hospital in Calcutta, after reading Elliotson's book, used hypnosis as an anaesthetic to control surgical pains. He performed more than a thousand operations using mesmeric procedure to produce insensitivity to pain. This was before the discovery of chemo-anaesthesia using chloroform, ether, and nitrous oxide. More than 300 of these were major operations, including 19 amputations. To his amazement, the mortality rate dropped from 50 per cent to 5 per cent.

On his return to England, Esdaile suffered a fate similar to Mesmer. He was tried by the British Medical Association for charlatanism and lost his license. It is interesting to note that during his trial one physician stated that the use of hypnotic anaesthesia was blasphemous. He argued that God intended people to suffer and that pain should be borne with Christian fortitude.[3]

Braid and the Rebirth of Hypnosis

Dr. James Braid (1795-1860), a Scottish physician and surgeon practising medicine in Manchester, deserves to be called the "father of modern hypnosis." He took animal magnetism out of the dark region of charlatanry and brought it into the clear domain of science. He coined the term *hypnotism*, derived from the Greek word *hypnos*, meaning sleep. In 1841, he attended a mesmeric demonstration by Lafontaine, a traveling Swiss mesmerist, in Manchester. Convinced that hypnotism was a fraud, Braid, attending the demonstration of eye catalepsy and analgesia, changed his opinion and began to investigate it.

James Braid then wrote *Neurypnology* (meaning "nervous sleep"), in which he gave the main exposition of his ideas about hypnosis. He originally believed that production of the hypnotic trance was caused by generating fatigue in the subject's eyes through his visual fixation on a small bright object. The fatigue of the eye muscles, Braid maintained, leads to a general fatigue which eventually affects the functioning of the nervous system and produces the hypnotic trance. For this reason, the induction is slowest when the eyes are directed straight ahead, and is fastest when they are concentrated upward on a hypnotic object slightly above the eye level. However, he later found that visual fixation was not necessary and that mental fixation on a particular thought or idea, suggested verbally, could produce the hypnotic state. One of the basic findings of Braid was that the hypnotic trance could be easily produced without going through induction rituals and formalities.

Braid believed that hypnotic phenomena were not due to the will of the magnetizer or any other mysterious agent that passed from the operator to the subject. On the contrary, he held that production of the mesmeric phenomenon was dependent upon the physical and psychological condition of the subject.

With time, Braid's theories progressed from the physiological to the psychological. And finally he came to the conclusion that, as had already been found by Abbe Faria and Alexander Bertrand, hypnotic phenomena were entirely subjective and that the hypnotist influenced the subject by suggestion and not by any physiological force. After this discovery and believing that hypnosis was not sleep, Braid attempted to replace the term *hypnosis* with the term *monoideism.** But he did not succeed. The term *hypnosis* was already in common use.

Liebeault and Bernheim, Demise of Animal Magnetism and Affirmation of Suggestion

In 1864 Ambroise A. Liebeault (1823-1904), a humble French physician working in a small village near Nancy, became interested in hypnosis after reading Braid's book *Neurypnology*. Liebeault, considered the "father of suggestive therapeutic hypnosis," moved to Nancy in eastern France and began to treat not only functional, but also organic diseases by hypnosis. Even though he was poverty-stricken, to avoid being called a charlatan, Liebeault would not charge the patients who agreed to be treated by hypnosis. Only if they wanted to be treated by drugs, would he charge his fee.

---

*The ability to think of one thing at a time so as to exclude all other ideas. In such a condition the organism reacts only to a single stimulus for a considerable length of time.

Liebeault believed that hypnosis was a valuable means not only for curing organic diseases, but also for the improvement of people's behavior. In 1866, he published the results of his treatments by hypnosis in a book entitled *Du Sommeil* .... Only one copy was sold.

Liebeault's contribution to hypnosis was not adequately recognized until 1895. At this time, Hippolyte Bernheim (1837-1919), a professor in the Medical School at Nancy, had been unsuccessfully treating a case of sciatica. This patient in desperation went to see Liebeault and was quickly cured by hypnotic suggestion.[4] Bernheim, originally wanting to expose Liebeault as a quack, became so fascinated by his method, that he became an ardent proponent of hypnotherapy and a devotee of Liebeault. Thereafter, Bernheim moved to Nancy and, with Liebeault, established the famous Nancy School of Hypnosis, where the patients (over 12,000 of them) were treated only by hypnosis.

Physicians from many countries flocked to Nancy to study Liebeault's and Bernheim's methods. Freud was one of those visitors. In 1884 Bernheim published his book *De La Suggestion* in which, like Braid, he considered suggestion to be the basis of the hypnotic state.

These two men believed that hypnosis was a psychological phenomenon rather than a physiological condition. They also maintained that symptom removal through hypnosis was harmless and an effective means for curing psychological disorders.

Liebeault and Bernheim had effectively revived the science of hypnosis.

Charcot and Momentary Revival of Animal Magnetism

By the end of the 19th century Dr. Jean-Martin Charcot (1825-1893), the greatest neurologist of his era, impressed by the demonstrations given by Donato, a Belgian stage hypnotist, began to experiment with hypnosis and give it a scientific basis. Because he had never hypnotized anyone himself and since he had worked only with three hysterical women, he thought that hypnosis was pathological, and that only hysterical people could be hypnotized. Thus once again, he tried to prove that hypnosis was based on an animal magnetic force.

Charcot believed that all hysterical symptoms, namely physical symptoms without any organic basis, such as paralysis, deafness, etc. could be both produced and eliminated by hypnosis.[5] He maintained that the hypnotic state could be produced by physical means and some hypnotic phenomena also could be induced and terminated by means of magnets and metals.[6]

While Liebeault and Bernheim believed that suggestion was the only basis of a hypnotic trance and that almost everyone was suggestible, Charcot believed that hypnosis was a form of hysteria, considered it a rare condition and did not appreciate the therapeutic value of hypnosis.

The controversy between the Charcot views (Salpetrier School of thought) and the theories of Bernheim (the Nancy School of thought), lasted for about ten years. But with the death of Charcot in 1893, the hypothesis of animal magnetism was refuted and the Nancy School of thought (psychological suggestion) which thought that hypnosis was based on suggestion was accepted. With this development, hypnosis became an effective tool of therapy.

Pierre Janet and the Theory of Dissociation

Pierre Janet (1859-1947), Charcot's student and a co-worker of Freud's, was appointed by Charcot as Director of the Psychological Laboratory at the Paris Hospital of Salpetrier. Like his teacher, Janet also linked hypnosis with hysteria but while Charcot emphasized the physiological principles, Janet laid greater stress on the psychological mechanism and developed his well-known theory of *dissociation*, in which one part of the mind functions separately from the others. For instance, during the hypnotic state the subject could be asked to recall things which he had forgotten in the waking state. On the other hand, he might be made to forget very simple things of which he was supposed to be well aware, for example, his name, a number, or a word.

Janet discovered that neurotic people will forget a great number of things especially if they are associated with repressed desires and unpleasant events. According to him, hypnosis is a mechanism which enables such memories to be brought back to consciousness, bringing relief to the subject. Janet believed that hypnosis could be used as an effective instrument for exploring the personality.

In short, Janet's contribution to the development of hypnosis made therapeutic suggestion a fully-fledged tool of medicine. What Janet predicted over 75 years ago that it will be tomorrow when there will be a new turn in fashion's wheel which will bring back hypnotism as surely as our grandmother's styles, is now becoming evident.[7]

Freud and the Dormancy of Hypnosis

Sigmund Freud (1856-1939), the pioneer of psychoanalysis, studied at Salpetrier and Nancy under Charcot, Liebeault and Bernheim, translated the latter's work on hypnotism into German, and even added a preface of his own. He also worked with Josef Breur (1842-1925), a general practitioner and one of the best medical hypnotists of that time. Prior to developing psychoanalysis, Freud used hypnosis to explore the unconscious mind of the mentally ill and to better understand the nature of their personalities. From his studies of hypnotism he developed the theory of psychoanalysis.

He was a firm believer in "psychic determinism" and discovered that recalling past memories and the resulting discharge of emotions could lead to the healing of the patient. But because of the misconceptions about hypnosis at that time and his own doubts, he abandoned hypnosis and devoted himself to the development of psychoanalysis, free association and dream induction.

Freud's misgivings about hypnosis came about, to a great extent, because of his experiences and difficulties with one patient (Lucie) in which he discovered that recall of past memories could be accomplished in the waking state as well as the hypnotic state. He mistakenly thought that a very deep stage of hypnosis was mandatory for therapeutic cure and, as a result, felt few patients were able to benefit from the process. In addition, Freud held a number of erroneous ideas in regard to the nature of hypnosis including the misconception that hypnosis was produced by the doctor and not by the patient (leaving the patient, he thought, stripped of any defenses). He also thought that post-hypnotic suggestion given during hypnosis would not be recalled upon awakening and insisted that hypnosis led to direct symptom removal which he believed to be a hindrance to permanent cure.[8]

Freud eventually came to believe that consciously uncovering the psychological causes of mental disorders (catharsis) was more helpful than unconsciously doing so and in his autobiography wrote: "Psychoanalysis only began with my rejection of the hypnotic technique."[9] However, Freud did not discredit the validity of hypnosis as an effective means of psychotherapy.

Because of his tremendous prestige, on the other hand, his rejection of hypnosis was a great blow to its use. His followers took this as sacred dogma and did not use hypnosis in their practices. As a result, hypnosis again was pushed back into the hands of quacks and stage hypnotists for half a century. Erickson stated: "The exploitation of hypnosis, a naturally occurring psycho-physiological phenomenon, as a demonstration of power, prestige, influence, and control (as in stage hypnosis), was a most unfortunate turn in the evolution of the history of hypnosis and the development of this faculty."

Had Freud shown interest in hypnosis, this phenomenon would today be tremendously developed.

Recent Developments

During World Wars I and II and the Korean War, "shell shock" or battle neuroses prompted a revival of hypnosis. A large number of victims were suffering from psychoneurosis caused by the trauma of war and there were not enough psychiatrists to deal with them. The medical authorities, searching for a short-cut form of therapy, generated a new interest in hypnosis and the result was more than satisfactory. In treating war neurotics, Hadfield originated the term *Hypnoanalysis* as a combination of hypnotic techniques and psychiatry. And hypnosis was used to treat thousands of war trauma stricken soldiers. The patients were hypnotized and made to associate their abreactions with healthy emotions.

In 1955, the British Medical Association became the first organization to formally approve the use of hypnosis in medical schools and post-graduate curricula.

In 1958, the American Medical Association followed suit and approved that instruction of hypnosis be included in medical schools and post-graduate curricula.

These positive developments indicate that hypnosis has finally become accepted as a valuable adjunct to medical and particularly psychological therapy.

REFERENCES

1. MacHovec, Frank J., *Exorcism: A Manual for Casting Out Evil Spirits* (New York: the Peter Pauper Press, 1973), p.6.
2. Rosen, George, "History of Medical Hypnosis" in *Hypnosis in Modern Medicine,* ed. Jerome Schneck (Springfield, IL: Charles C. Thomas Publishers), p. 19.
3. Cheek, David B. and Leslie M. LeCron, *Clinical Hypnotherapy* (New York: Grune & Stratton, 1968), p. 17.
4. Bramwell, Milne, *Hypnotism* (London: Wm. Rider & Sons, 1913), p.30.
5. Udolf, Roy, *Handbook of Hypnosis for Professionals* (New York: Van Nostrand Reinhold Co., 1981), p. 7.
6. Schneck, Jerome, *Hypnosis in Modern Medicine* (Springfield, IL: Charles C. Thomas Publishers, 1953), p. 23.
7. Michaluk, Wladyslaw, *Understanding Hypnosis: A Brief Guide* (Washington, D.C.: Hypnos Press, 1981), p.9.
8. Kroger, William S. and William D. Fezler, *Hypnosis and Behavior Modification: Imagery Conditioning* (Philadelphia: J. B. Lippincott Co.), p.9.
9. Freud, Sigmund, *Autobiography,* trans. J. Strachey (New York: W.W. Norton and Co., Inc., 1953), p.48.

CHAPTER TWO

MISCONCEPTIONS ABOUT HYPNOSIS

The layman often has various misconceptions about hypnosis. The hypnotist should try to remove these erroneous ideas in the pre-induction talk and before attempting the induction process. The most common of these misconceptions are outlined below.

Hypnosis is Sleep

In the popular mind hypnosis is often equated with sleep. There are a number of reasons for this. Firstly, there is the rather unfortunate choice by Braid of the term *hypnosis* from the Greek word for sleep *hypnos*. Further, Pavlov linked sleep to hypnosis. He believed that the connection between sleep and hypnosis was cortical inhibition, which he maintained might manifest itself as either sleep or hypnosis. Of course, the observations which led to this theory were made while working with conditioned reflexes in dogs. Finally, and most importantly, there is the superficial similarity between sleep and hypnosis. The fact that during hypnosis the subject closes his eyes, breathes quietly and regularly, and has some alterations in his consciousness, leads people into thinking that the subject is asleep. Indeed there are many hypnotists and hypnotherapists who perpetuate the myth by using "sleep" terminology.

In spite of the superficial similarity between a hypnotic trance and natural sleep, the two states are completely different psychologically as well as physiologically. The differences between the hypnotic trance and natural sleep are as follows:

1. In natural sleep, focal awareness (consciousness) is bypassed; in the hypnotic trance it is intensified. In the hypnotized state both the conscious and unconscious minds of the subject are combined and work together (with the unconscious mind having the dominant role), while in natural sleep only the unconscious mind is active. Of course, the deeper a subject goes under trance, the more his unconscious mind takes over his conscious mind.*

2. In natural sleep, unlike the hypnotic state, a person does not hear or respond to vocal instructions or suggestions.

3. In natural sleep, the knee jerk (the patellar reflex) is greatly diminished and in some cases entirely absent; during hypnosis the knee will react normally.[2]

4. If natural sleep and hypnosis were the same, then one might go more easily into hypnosis from sleep than from a waking state. This relationship has not been proven, nor has the effect of suggestion been shown to be active during sleep, as it is in the hypnotic trance.

5. During natural sleep limbs become flaccid from lack of

---

*Electroencephalograph (EEG) studies have shown that alpha activity is higher during the hypnotic trance. Alpha is described as the noise that the brain makes when it is alert and resting. It is inconsistent with the EEG patterns observed during sleep.[1]

activity. In the hypnotic state, they can be made rigid and stiff. During normal sleep a person is not able to hold anything in his hand, but in the hypnotic state he can grasp an object for any length of time.

6. Cardiac (heart) and respiratory (lungs) action during hypnosis is nearer to that of the waking state than to normal sleep.[3]

7. Blood circulation during hypnosis resembles that of the waking state rather than that of sleep.[4]

8. The basal rate of metabolism (i.e. man's metabolism in the resting state) is decreased from ten to fifteen per cent during natural sleep, but such a decrease is not seen with hypnosis.[5]

It is apparent, therefore, that although outwardly hypnosis resembles natural sleep, the actual state of hypnosis is in no way related to sleep. It is difficult to come to any conclusion other than that sleep is not hypnosis and that hypnosis is neither a suggested sleep nor a modified sleep, nor anything between sleep and the normal waking state.

Only Weakminded People Are Hypnotizable

The idea that unintelligent or weakminded people are more hypnotizable than intelligent people is completely false, and tests have shown that those of higher intelligence are more easily hypnotized. This myth existed as a result of a debate between Charcot and Bernheim. The former believed that only hysterics were hypnotizable, while the latter maintained that a person's capacity to be hypnotized was in no way a sign of mental deficiency.

Recent data illustrates that hypnotic capacity is a sign of relative mental health and that morons, imbeciles, weak-

minded people and severely disturbed patients are incapable
of a hypnotic trance. Practical experiments and scientific
research have proven that people of above average intelligence, who are capable of concentrating, are more susceptible to hypnosis.[6] However, the ability to concentrate, is a
necessary but not per se a sufficient condition for hypnotic
susceptibility, because some people who have good concentration are relatively unsusceptible.[7]

Marcuse states: "In one empirical study it was found that
volunteers for hypnosis possessed higher intelligence, had less
anxiety, were more (not less) dominant, and were less prejudiced in general than non-volunteers."[8] This is not sur-
prising because hypnosis depends on the understanding and
cooperation of the subject. An intelligent mind responds to
logic and reason and cooperates more during the trance
induction procedure. According to Bernhardt and Martin:
"The best subjects tend to be those of average or above
average intelligence, possessed of strong motivation and the
ability to concentrate."[9]

The Hypnotist Should Have a Dominant Personality

According to this idea, a hypnotist should have a strong,
dominant, dynamic personality. Therefore, men, having
supposedly dominant personalities are better hypnotists
than women.

This is only a myth. Because all hypnosis is self-hypnosis,
the subject, and not the hypnotist, is responsible for the
induction of the hypnotic trance. Thus the receptivity
of the subject and his motivation are more important than
the personality of the hypnotist. The stage hypnotist tries to
give the impression that his all-powerful person produces hyp-

nosis. For this reason, he administers striking passes, he gesticulates, has a fixed stare during the induction procedure and generally tries to demonstrate that his mystical procedure produces hypnosis. The crucial role of the subject is correspondingly minimized. Such pretensions merely obscure the fact that hypnosis occurs as a result of the subject's cooperation, imagination and expectation.[10] Of course, the rapport of the hypnotist with the subject is also a positive factor and it has a tremendous effect on a successful hypnotic trance.

Danger of Not Being Dehypnotized

The danger that subject may not be awakened from the hypnotic trance is extremely rare but popularly exaggerated. Most hypnotists would affirm that they rarely encounter the slightest difficulty in awakening a subject from a hypnotic trance. This point has been thouroughly discussed under "dehypnotization."

Loss of Control, Revelation of Secrets and Committing Anti-Social Acts

Some believe that during hypnosis they will lose self-control, reveal intimate secrets, and commit anti-social acts. In this context, it should be noted that subjects are not dominated by the will of the hypnotist, but are in full control of themselves, fully aware of their environment, and completely capable of making decisions at all times. If a subject is directly asked to commit an action which is objectionable to him, he will simply reject doing it, and in some cases he will be awakened from the trance. Milton

Erickson states that the hypnotic relationship is analogous to that between physician and patient, lawyer and client, or minister or parishioner. The danger of dependency is no greater with hypnosis than without it.[11] However, an unscrupulous hypnotist by producing a total amnesia, appealing to a genuine, hidden desire and using hallucination can make a subject already predisposed to lie, steal, or kill, commit a criminal or anti-social act. Hypnosis can then be used as an alibi, a rationalization, or legitimization of behavior.[12]

Although a hypnotist does not have complete control over a subject, his words can be more influential than they would be if the subject were not hypnotized. On the other hand, people can influence the behavior of other people by their suggestions whether their listeners are hypnotized or not. Yet it is true that words can be more devastating than bacteria and have the power to cure or harm whether the listener is hypnotized or not.

Hypnosis is Harmful

Hypnosis per se cannot be considered harmful in any way, unless it is applied by an inexperienced hypnotist. Hypnosis is a valid scientific phenomenon which can help people overcome mental problems. "The mere induction of hypnosis without suggestion may lead to improvement."[13] While hypnosis is of itself a relaxing and soothing experience and will not produce any physical or mental disorder, it can be abused. If a stage hypnotist causes a subject to go through some emotionally upsetting experiences, then this may lead to problems. Here the danger is not the hypnosis, but its mismanagement.

Some people think that constant hypnotic induction

weakens the mind. On the contrary hypnosis refreshes the mind and relieves tension. Millions of people have been hypnotized hundreds of times without the faintest sign of harm. There are also some other myths about hypnosis, such as being helpless to resist undesirable post-hypnotic suggestions. Before trance induction in the pre-induction talk, the hypnotist has to remove all doubts and misconceptions about hypnosis. Establishing a good rapport with the subject and easing fear will help facilitate a successful hypnotic induction.

REFERENCES

1. Spiegel, H. and D. Spiegel, *Trance and Treatment: Clinical Uses of Hypnosis* (New York, Basic Books, Inc., 1978), p. 15.
2. Bass, Milton J., "Differentiation of the Hypnotic Trance from Natural Sleep," *Journal of Experimental Psychology*, 14:382-99, 1931.
3. Jennes, Arthur and Charles L. Wible, "Electrocardiograms during Sleep and Hypnosis," *Journal of Psychology*, 1:235-245, 1936; Jenness and Wible, "Respiration and Heart Action in Sleep and Hypnosis," *Journal of General Psychology*, 16:197-222, 1937.
4. Nyard, Wallace J., "Cerebral Circulation Prevailing During Sleep and Hypnosis," *Psychological Bulletin*, 34:272, 1937.
5. Teitelbaum, M., *Hypnosis Induction Techniques* (Springfield, IL.: Charles C. Thomas Publishers, 1978), p. 9.
6. Hilgard, J. R., "Imaginative Involvement: Some Characteristics of the Highly Hypnotizable and the Non-Hypnotizable," *International Journal of Clinical & Experimental Hypnosis*, 22,138-56, 1974.
7. Van Nuys, D., "Meditation, Attention, and Hypnotic Susceptibility: A Correlational Study," *International Journal of Clinical and Experimental Hypnosis*, 21: 59-69, 1973.
8. Marcuse, F. L., *Hypnosis: Fact and Fiction* (London: Penguin Books, 1976), p. 91.
9. Bernhardt, R. and D. Martin, *Self-Mastery Through Self-Hypnosis* (New York: The Bobbs-Merrill Co., Inc., 1977), p. 28.
10. Schneck, J. M., "Relationship Between Hypnotist-Audience and Hypnotist-Subject Interaction," *International Journal of Clinical and Experimental Hypnosis*, 6:171, 1958.
11. Erickson, M., "Hypnosis in Medicine," *Medical Clinics of North America*, 28:639, 1944.
12. Kroger, W. S., *Clinical and Experimental Hypnosis* (Philadelphia: J. B. Lippincott Co., 1977), p. 99.
13. Marcuse, *Hypnosis: Fact and Fiction*, p. 123.

CHAPTER THREE

THE NATURE AND PROPERTIES OF HYPNOSIS

Hull said: "All sciences alike have descended from magic and superstition, but none has been so slow as hypnosis in shaking off the evil associations of its origin."[1] Indeed, no science has ever had so many ups and downs in its evolution as hypnosis. It is one of the oldest sciences yet it is the least known of all the sciences. Today more than 300 years after the beginning of modern or scientific hypnosis, despite the contributions of so many devoted scientists, we are still not completely aware of all the various aspects of hypnosis.

Josef B. Rhine, internationally known researcher of psychic phenomena at Duke University has said: "It is shocking that we know the atom today better than we know the mind that knows the atom."[2] But in understanding hypnosis, which is one of the most vivid manifestations of the mind, we we are even more backward. The question, "What is hypnosis?", remains unanswered.

There are almost as many definitions and theories concerning the nature of hypnosis as there are hypnotists. Scientists of every field try to have theories to work with, but at present we can only describe hypnosis rather than theorize correctly about it. Hypnosis, thus, can be called a *de facto* rather than a *de jure* state of science.

There is a tremendous literature on hypnosis, but it is often contradictory. Most views of hypnosis, however, can be divided into either the physiological or the psychological school of thought. The physiological school views hypnosis as an altered condition of the brain, while the psychological contingent sees it as a unique interpersonal relationship. Some theorists have tried to combine the two points of view but the two parts of the theory remain discrete. Charcot described hypnosis as a state of hysteria.[3] He believed that only hysterical individuals were hypnotizable. White[4] and Dorcus[5] thought that hypnosis was goal oriented behavior. The subject fulfills expectations and behaves like a hypnotized subject. Most authorites—including Bernheim, Hull, and Weitzenhoffer—believed hypnosis to be a form of selective hypersuggestibility.[6] Hull[7] has concluded that hypersuggestibility follows the same laws as habit. Spiegel[8] interpreted hypnosis as a psychophysiological state of aroused, attentive, receptive focal concentration with an associating dullness of awareness. Meares[9] thought that hypnosis was an atavistic regression to a more primitive level of functioning—in other words, a primordial mental process which determined the acceptance of ideas, prior to man's acquisition of the ability to logical thought. Van Pelt[10] thought that hypnosis was a superconcentration of the mind. Salter[11] regarded hypnosis as a learned phenomenon, or a form of conditioning. Sarbin and Coe[12] suggested that hypnosis was the result of role-playing. Erickson wrote about hypnosis as selective perception—a process in which the subject chooses to see only what is relevant to his task and blocks out everything else. In this way, daydreaming is a form of hypnosis. Meditation is another form; so is watching a favorite television program, a captivating film, or reading an engrossing book. "Waking hypnosis," in fact, occurs in the course of our everyday existence. It occurs when the attention span is heightened and suggestibility increased. On the other hand, it has been argued that hypnosis is like natural sleep because in both states the unconscious mind takes over the mentality of the person. Since the brain can develop negative and positive hallucinations during dreams, it can develop such phenomena during hypnosis also. The phenomena of hypnosis occur whenever reality is made of unreality.

Pavlov[13] believed that hypnosis was a partial sleep or a special excitation of certain cerebral regions and relative depressions of the other zones of the brain. Barber[14] contended that hypnosis was a non-state phenomenon. He has given an interesting interpretation of the nature of hypnosis. He compares the unresponsive hypnotic subject and the responsive hypnotic subject to two persons watching a stage play or movie. The highly responsive or good subject resembles that member of the audience who experiences the thoughts, feelings and sensations that the actors are attempting to arouse. He lets himself imagine, think about and experience the suggested effects, such as joy, fear, and anger. The unresponsive or poor subject, on the other hand, resembles that member of the audience who observes but does not sympathetically experience the thoughts, feelings, and emotions that the actors are attempting to arouse. The unresponsive subject does not let himself imagine and accept suggested affects.

Rabkin[15] also says a person seeing a good show is hypnotized whenever he forgets he is part of the audience, and

instead feels he is a part of the story. The bottomline concept all the authors' ideas mentioned above is that the individual who is engrossed or totally absorbed in a movie,
book, or play is not really concentrating. He is not forcing
himself to pay attention to the subject. The attentiveness
experienced comes automatically and without critical attention.

Janet [16] regarded the artificially produced hypnosis as a
condition of *dissociation*. Gill and Brenman[17] thought that
hypnosis was an adaptive regression. Freud[18] defined hypnosis as a transference phenomenon. He considered hypnosis
a love relationship contending that there is an erotic relationship between the hypnotist and the subject. He believed
that hypnosis is like "being in love" with sexual satisfaction
excluded. Orne,[19] Hilgard,[20] Kroger,[21] and many others
finally came to the conclusion that hypnosis was a "state"
or "trance." Orne [22] maintained that the hypnotic subject
develops a tolerance for logical inconsistencies, what he called
"trance logic."

Wolberg [23] was apparently the first to propose that hypnosis is psychosomatic, i.e., both physiological and psychological in character.

There is, however, a widely held view that hypnosis is
not a state of unconsciousness, sleep, or trance; rather it is
an exaggerated state of awareness. [24]

Definition of Hypnosis

Due to the polymorphous nature of hypnosis and the dis-
agreements among hypnotist scholars about its reality, there
is no consensus on its definition.

Cooke and Vogt state: "Present day knowledge of hypnosis might be roughly compared to the knowledge of electricity half a century ago. The electron was unknown and so it was impossible to define electricity as a flow of electrons through a conducting material. And yet, though no definition was possible, a mighty science and a mighty industry were growing and new uses for electricity were discovered daily. It might be said, therefore, that some as yet undiscovered psychological or physiological or psychophysiological (electron) may give us, in time, a theory of hypnosis which will account for all the observed phenomena. At present we must be content to say that we do not know *what it is,* but we are beginning to understand how it works."[25]

Meanwhile we must settle for a working definition. I offer the following: *Hypnosis is a particular altered state of selective hypersuggestibility brought about in an individual by the use of a combination of relaxation, fixation of attention, and suggestion.*

This definition is in line with both Weitzenhoffer's interpretation of the nature of hypnosis and Gindes' subjective oriented formula of hypnosis. Weizenhoffer states that man is an organism that reacts to his environment mainly through his neuromuscular apparatus. Man is stimulated nearly entirely, through direct and indirect action on his nerve endings or his receptors. All effective stimulation leads to a response and nearly all responses especially those initiated by stimuli from his external environment, are meditated by his nervous system.[26]

Gindes who tends to rely more on the subjective approach rather than the objective approach to hypnotic induction, offers the following fixed formula for hypnosis: "Misdirected attention + belief + expectation= hypnosis."[27] He believes that imagination is the integrative factor that welds belief and expectation into an irresistable force.

REFERENCES

1. Hull, Clark L., *Hypnosis and Suggestibility* (New York: Appleton-Century Crofts, Inc., 1933), p. 18.
2. Brown, M., "New Evidence on Psychic Phenomena," *Reader's Digest*, May, 1981, p. 113.
3. Schneck, *Hypnosis in Modern Medicine*, p. 23.
4. White, R. W., "A Preface to the Theory of Hypnotism," *Journal of Abnormal and Social Psychology*, 36: 477, 1941.
5. Dorcus, R. M., "Modification by Suggestion of Some Vestibular and Visual Responses," *American Journal of Psychology*, 49: 82-87, 1937.
6. Estabrooks, G. H., *Hypnotism* (New York: Dutton, 1943), p. 130.
7. Hull, *Hypnosis and Suggestibility*, p. 344-348.
8. Spiegel, *Trance and Treatment.*
9. Meares, A., *A System of Medical Hypnosis* (Philadelphia: W. B. Saunders, 1960)
10. Van Pelt, *Secrets of Hypnotism*, p. 4.
11. Salter, A., *What is Hypnosis* (New York: Richard R. Smith, 1944), p. 36.
12. Sarbin, T. R. and William Coe, *Hypnosis: A Social Psychological Analysis of Influence Communication* (New York: Holt, Rinehart and Winston, Inc., 1972), p. 63.
13. Pavlov, I. P., "The Identity of Inhibition with Sleep and Hypnosis," *Scientific Monthly*, 17: 603-608, 1923.
14. Barber, T. X., "Suggested (Hypnotic) Behavior: The Trance Paradigm Versus an Alternative Paradigm," in *Hypnosis: Research Developments and Perspectives*, ed. E. Fromm and R. E. Shor (Chicago: Aldine-Atherton, Inc., 1972), pp. 119-122.
15. Rabkin, R., *Strategic Psychotherapy: Brief and Symptematic Treatment* (New York: Basic Books, 1977), p. 230.
16. Janet, P., *Principles of Psychotherapy*, trans. E. R. Guthrie (New York: Freeport, 1971), pp. 131-133.
17. Gill, M. M. and M. Brenman, *Hypnosis and Related States* (New York: International University Press, 1959), p. xxiii.
18. Freud, S., *Group Psychology and the Analysis of the Ego*, trans. J. Strachey (New York: W. W. Norton and Co., Inc., 1959), p. 47.
19. Orne, M., "Hypnosis, Motivation and Compliance," *American Journal of Psychiatry*, 122: 721-26, 1966.
20. Hilgard, J. R., *Personality and Hypnosis* (Chicago: University of Chicago Press, 1970), p. 247.
21. Kroger, *Clinical and Experimental Hypnosis*, p. 28.
22. Orne, M. T., "The Nature of Hypnosis: Artifact and Essence," *Journal of Abnormal and Social Psychology*, 58: 277-99, 1959.
23. Wolberg, L. R., *Medical Hypnosis, 2 Vols.* (New York: Grune & Stratton, Inc., 1948), 1:82.

24. Kroger and Fezler, *Hypnosis and Behavior Modification*, pp. 14-15.
25. Cooke, C. E. and A. E. Van Vogt, *The Hypnotism Handbook* (Alhambra, Ca.: Borden Publishing Co., 1965), p. 54.
26. Weitzenhoffer, A., *Hypnotism: An Objective Study in Suggestibility* (New York: John Wiley & Sons, Inc., 1953), p. 278.
27. Gindes, B. C., *New Concepts of Hypnosis* (Hollywood, CA., Wilshire Book Co., 1951), p. 77.

CHAPTER FOUR

SUSCEPTIBILITY TO HYPNOSIS

People are naturally susceptible to hypnosis. In theory, every normal person could be hypnotized under proper conditions by an experienced hypnotist. In actual practice, however, a small percentage of people cannot be induced into the hypnotic trance. While there are some people who enter a very deep trance very quickly on the first induction, others—even those willing to be hypnotized—may only reach a light trance on repeated attempts at hypnosis.

Although susceptibility to hypnosis seems to be a natural characteristic of people, it may be neutralized in many ways. If a physician suggests hypnotherapy to his emotionally ill patient, the patient will usually show a great desire to be hypnotized; he wishes to cure himself and the doctor has legitimized hypnosis. Yet despite being highly motivated, the subject may not be susceptible to hypnosis. On the other hand, a hypnotizable person who is forced into therapy by a member of his family or a friend but is not willing to relinquish his habit (for instance, smoking), may not be hypnotized. The former (who is consciously willing to be hypnotized but is not hypnotizable) is described as consciously willing but unconsciously unwilling. The latter (who is unwilling to be hypnotized but is found to be hypnotizable) is described as consciously unwilling but unconsciously willing.

Therefore, it can be said that the most significant factor in susceptibility to hypnosis is the motivation to be hypnotizable. Over-cooperativeness and over-anxiousness to be hypnotized, however, are counterproductive and make a hypnotic trance difficult to reach. An unconscious motivation to be hypnotized may be stronger than the conscious will to resist hypnosis. For this reason, if a person consciously resists hypnosis, he will finally find it difficult to stay awake and will drift into the hypnotic trance (The Law of Reversed Effect).

But passive subjects are clearly the most easily hypnotized. Laboratory studies of susceptibility to hypnosis have been contradictory and are therefore unreliable. From the results of thousands of reported cases we can, however, make a rough estimate that about 5 to 20 per cent of people reach the deepest hypnotic depth and that another 5 to 20 per cent are not at all susceptible to hypnosis. The remaining 60 to 90 per cent are said to be capable of entering light to medium hypnosis.[1]

For a more detailed and concrete analysis of proneness to hypnosis, the above figures may be examined along with other demographic factors, such as age, sex, intelligence, occupation, and personality.

Age

In general, children under six or seven years old are difficult subjects because of their poor understanding of both language and verbal induction procedures. Seven year-olds and above tend to be good subjects and their susceptibility seems to increase to a maximum in the 9 to 14 year-old age range. The period from 14 to 21 years old is the best period both for speed of induction and depth of hypnosis, but of course the two, speed of induction and depth of hypnosis, are not necessarily related. From 20 years on, there is a gradual decline in susceptibility to hypnosis. People over the age of 75 are generally poor subjects even though there are exceptions. Sometimes even a child may be very resistant, while an 80 year-old person may be a good subject and produce a very deep trance. The general rule is that there are fewer good subjects in the older age groups, but this can vary greatly with the individual.

Sex

Popular opinion indicates that women are more susceptible to hypnosis than men. But the literature on hypnotism unanimously rejects this idea and regards the hypnotic capacity of males and females as equal. LeCron believes that this misconception about women being more susceptible stems from the fact that they are usually more willing to be hypnotized, perhaps more curious, and less afraid than the so-called "braver" male.[2] Udolf maintains that such a misconception "may have resulted from the more passive social role of women, combined with the idea that in hypnosis a dominant hypnotist controls a passive subject."[3]

At any rate, the research in general indicates that men and women are completely equal in susceptibility to hypnosis.

Intelligence

There seems to be some correlation between intelligence and susceptibility to hypnosis. A good hypnotic subject should be able to concentrate properly and follow the instructions of the hypnotist and this needs a certain minimal amount of intelligence.

Because the capacity for hypnosis is actually in the subject and all forms of hypnosis are really self-hypnosis it becomes important that the subject have a good mind—even more important than the qualities of the hypnotist. Arons states: "It is fairly safe to say that a person with an IQ of 70 or less is not hypnotizable."[4]

Feebleminded individuals are not susceptible to hypnosis because of their inherent mental deficiency and also their inability to communicate properly.

In brief, persons with a real intellectual deficiency make poor hypnotic subjects and foil the ingenuity of the hypnotist.

Occupation

Occupation seems to bear a positive correlation with susceptibility to hypnosis. Arons[5] has dealt with this point in detail and believes that people engaged in monotonous or routine jobs, e.g. factory and assembly line workers, are very susceptible to hypnosis. The reason being that, firstly, they perform the same motion or series of motions at a machine throughout the day and, secondly, their minds appear to get into a static mental cycle.

Those who are accustomed to issuing orders to subordinates, such as army officers, seem to be difficult subjects.

For the same reason those accustomed to being submissive to orders, such as soldiers, sailors, and domestics, make good hypnotic subjects. Religious people (particularly fanatical ones) who are capable of suspending critical judgement are also good subjects.

Engineers, scientific workers (such as computer programers), and those analytically and scientifically minded, who believe that everything should conform to certain physical laws are poor hypnotic subjects. Writers, artists, and other imaginative people tend to be susceptible to hypnosis.

"Dr. Hilgard found humanities majors most susceptible to hypnosis, social science majors next, and science and engineering students least hypnotizable."[6]

Personality

A vast number of studies have been done to establish the relationship between personality and susceptibility to hypnosis. This research indicates that there is some correlation between personality or traits of character and susceptibility to hypnosis. It has been found that introverts tend to be slightly more susceptible than extroverts.[7] Exhibitionists, except those who use resistance as a device to show their exhibitory character, are good hypnotic subjects. Imbeciles, morons, paranoids, and senile persons, as mentioned before, are difficult if not impossible subjects.

There is some disagreement in the literature concerning the susceptibility of neurotics to hypnosis, but the general opinion is that there is little if any difference between them and non-neurotics regarding susceptibility to hypnosis.[8]

Contrary to the popular view, the results of relevant studies on hysteria do not show any link between hysteria and susceptibility to hypnosis.[9] A regressed schizophrenic is a poor hypnotic subject because it is difficult for the hypnotist to make contact and the subject's ability to concentrate is poor.[10]

Wilcox and Faw found that highly hypnotizable subjects were better adjusted. Those who showed signs of depression, insecurity, and distraction by bizarre thoughts and feelings were less well-adjusted.[11]

An interesting study by Rosenzweig and Sarason [12] shows that susceptibility to hypnosis is a personality trait of "impunitive" persons. Impunitive people are those who repress (exclude unacceptable ideas from consciousness) as a reaction to their frustration, and avoid aggressive behavior. "Impunitiveness" means the tendency to blame neither others (extrapunitive), nor themselves (intropunitive), but to find a logical reason. The essence of this hypothesis is that susceptibility to hypnosis has a positive correlation to repression and Impunitiveness, while non-hypnotizability is associated with projection,* intropunitiveness, and extrapunitiveness.

---

*A defense mechanism in which an anxiety-producing thought is projected onto another person. For instance, instead of saying, "I hate him," one says, "he hates me."

REFERENCES

1. Marcuse, *Hypnosis: Fact and Fiction,* p. 78.
2. LeCron, L. M. and J. Bordeaux, *Hypnotism Today* (No. Hollywood, CA.: Wilshire Book Co., 1947), p.77.
3. Udolf, *Handbook of Hypnosis for Professionals,* p.33.
4. Arons, H., *New Master Course in Hypnotism* (So.Orange, NJ.: Power Publishers, 1961), p. 50.
5. *Ibid.,* pp. 52-53.
6. Bernhardt and Martin, *Self-Mastery through Self-Hypnosis,* p. 18.
7. McDougall, W., *Outline of Abnormal Psychology* (New York: Scribner, 1962).
8. Udolf, *Handbook of Hypnosis for Professionals,* p. 36.
9. *Ibid.,* p. 37.
10. *Ibid.*
11. Wilcox, W. W. and V. Faw, "Social and Environmental Perceptions of Susceptible and Unsusceptible Hypnotic Subjects," *International Journal of Clinical & Experimental Hypnosis,* 7: 151-59.
12. Rosenzwig and Sarason, "An Experimental Study of the Triadic Hypothesis in Relation to Frustration, Ego-Defense, and Hypnotic Ability," *Character and Citizenship,* 11: 1-14, 150-65, 1942.

CHAPTER FIVE

CONCENTRATION OF THE MIND AND HYPNOSIS

Concentration of the mind is essential for hypnotic induction. If a person cannot concentrate his mind, he can neither be hypnotized, nor can he practice hypnosis. The mind can focus its attention on only one specific matter at a time. A person cannot properly read, talk, and listen to the radio at the same time, because each detracts from the other. In the same way, if the attention of a subject is divided he will not be able to go under a trance.

This power of concentration, vital in hypnosis, can also have an enormous impact on a person's everyday life. The early Judeo-Christian traditions taught that man must work to hear God's voice, using fasting and meditation to achieve the necessary "emptiness." Concentration of the mind is the first step towards mind control, without which we cannot achieve our goals. Concentration of the mind makes us masters of our fate and enables us to realize our long-held dreams. Dr. S. J. Van Pelt, former president of the British Society of Medical Hypnosis, a leading authority in medical hypnosis, states: "Genius is the result of the ability to superconcentrate the mind, and so make use of practically all the mind power available." He believes that any average person is a potential genius; anatomically there is no difference between the brain of the average person and the greatest genius. There is, however, a vast difference in the way they use their minds.[1]

The role of "thought," and particularly concentration of the mind, in developing the overall mental and bodily capacity of man has been generally underrated. Yet Plato said, "We become what we contemplate." And Christ said, "As a man thinketh, so he is."[2] An observation made by Dr. Gindes, a leading authority in hypnosis, can help us better understand the mechanism of "thought" in a person's life:

> Thought, basically, is the mainspring of all human existence. It is the foundation of every idea. Bridges are built, canvases painted, books written—all as a result of thought. It is the stimulus of every aggression, of every submission. Millions of years ago it was a thought which started primitive man on the long pathway to civilization.
> A thought can cause a man to give or to steal, to kill or to heal. Culprit or saint, man must be motivated by one thought or by a cluster of thoughts . . .
> We have learned, too, that thoughts may control the functions of the human body. They can cause changes in temperature, make us perspire or break out into goose-flesh. They can alter the regularity of a heart-beat, or the rate of blood-pressure and respiration. A fear thought compels the blood to leave the brain; if severe enough the victim faints. Psychosomatics, a branch of medical science that recognizes a mental basis for physical ailments, makes the bold assertion that eighty-five per cent of illnesses, hitherto regarded as organic, are actually functional in origin, i. e., they result directly from the impact upon the body of a thought charged with emotion . . . ." [3]

In embarking on any kind of activity, we can be a hundred times more successful if we concentrate. During meals, for example, our food can be digested more easily and quickly if we concentrate on eating rather than dividing our attention between eating and watching television or reading a book. The ability to concentrate is a prerequisite for a successful hypnotic state; and concentration can be strengthened under hypnosis.

Van Pelt[4] states that modern research has revealed that it may be possible for a person of average ability to develop positive genius under the influence of hypnosis. He explains that brain-wave tests carried out on Einstein confirm the theory that genius is associated with the ability to superconcentrate the mind. He quotes Cooper and Erickson who relate the case of the artist who had tried to paint a picture for ten years without success. Then under the influence of hypnotic suggestion the artist painted the picture in six hours which would have normally taken seventy hours.

In another part of his work, Van Pelt[5] cites the case of Sergei Rachmaninoff. Rachmaninoff was a great Russian musician whose First Symphony was played at St. Petersburg in 1897; it was a dismal failure and brought him severe criticism. Depressed at such a great failure, he was unable to write a new concerto. Even the advice of the great Tolstoy, whom Rachmaninoff deeply admired, was of no avail. However, a Dr. Dahl, using hypnosis, helped him to overcome his mental torpor. Rachmaninoff had daily treatment from January to April 1900, and before the end of the year he had completed two movements of the Concerto. As a result, Rachmaninoff achieved great success.

Concentration of the mind is a learned process and, like any other specific kind of behavior modification, can be developed. To develop the power of concentration, one has to concentrate deliberately and consistently.

The concept of "ideo-motor action" formulated by William James, indicates that whenever the attention is concentrated long enough on a thought or idea, it results in a physical action. Spontaneous concentration of the mind on a thought or idea is more effective in bringing about a physical action than simple or direct persuasion. When the mind concentrates spontaneously on an idea, the critical sensors or resistances to acceptance of a thought are bypassed and the idea is uncritically accepted and realized in physical activity. William James wrote: "The greatest discovery of my generation is that human beings can alter their lives by altering their attitudes of mind."[6] In the early part of the 20th century Edmund Jacobson, a physiologist at Harvard University, measured the action currents in muscles and discovered that a thought related to muscular activities could stimulate action currents in the appropriate muscles.

Given that the brain consists of 13 billion cells, that the number of possible circuits in the brain is greater than the number of atoms in the universe, and that no human being—even the most brilliant—has used more than 10 per cent of his mind in daily life, it follows that our minds have the potential to be trained much more easily than other parts of the body. Concentration of the mind is the key to this learning process.

How to Improve Concentration

The method that the author usually uses to teach his students how to develop the power of concentration is as follows:

1. The students are asked to relax their bodies, close their eyes, and make their minds blank. They are further instructed to keep their eyes closed until a thought finally insists upon coming into their minds and their concentration

is interrupted, in which case, they are to open their eyes. *(This exercise does not last more than 5 seconds for the average individual).*

2. The students are asked in the second exercise to focus exclusively on an object such as a doorknob, a spot on the wall, a tree in a picture hanging on the wall, etc. The students are then advised to open their eyes only when their concentration is interrupted by a persistent, intruding thought. Generally, the students are able to concentrate their minds for at least 30 seconds, i. e. six times more than in the first exercise.

3. In the third exercise, I put an hour-glass on a desk and ask the students to close their eyes and concentrate their attention on the individual grains of sand filtering down from the upper compartment of the hour-glass into the lower one. I further instruct the students that if in their imaginations they come to the point where all the grains of sand in the upper part of the hour-glass have fallen into the lower part, they should imagine that I have turned the hour-glass upside down. This process can be repeated endlessly in the subject's imagination.

This practice has been so effective in helping the students concentrate that after about a minute of giving relaxation suggestions, I have been able to put almost all of the students under trance, some very deeply.

The students in the first exercise could not concentrate their minds for more than five seconds because I did not assign them an object on which to focus their attention. In the second exercise they could concentrate their minds an average of six times more than in the first—for the simple reason that they had something to hold their attention. But in the third exercise, because the students were supposed to concentrate their attention on a moving object, they were able to focus their attention for a long time— longer than the second exercise and much longer than the first exercise—and were even able to go involuntarily under trance.

This series of exercises shows that the best way to improve the power of concentration is to practice focusing one's attention on a moving object and following the movement of its parts with the mental eye.

Another variation of this exercise is to close one's eyes and focus attention on the movements of the hands of an imaginary clock hanging on the wall, or imagine a bird is flying over the trees of a park, flying from one tree to the next. To perform these exercises, one has to be sure to limit one's attention to imaginary scenery, and not permit one's thoughts to wander.

If this exercise is carried out three times a day everyday for two weeks, the power of concentration will be considerably improved and mental productivity enhanced.

REFERENCES

1. Van Pelt, *Secrets of Hypnotism,* pp. 140-41.
2. Tebbetts, C., *Self-Hypnosis and other Mind Expanding Techniques* (Los Angeles, CA.: Westwood Publishing Co., 1977), p. 11.
3. Gindes, *New Concepts of Hypnosis,* p. 4.
4. Van Pelt, *Secrets of Hypnotism,* pp. 140-41.
5. *Ibid.,* p. 96.
6. Bernhardt and Martin, *Self-Mastery Through Self-Hypnosis.*

CHAPTER SIX

UNCONSCIOUS MIND AND HYPNOSIS

Granted that the unconscious mind has a great role in hypnosis, particularly in the effectiveness of post-hypnotic suggestions, it is relevant to have a look first at the unconscious mind itself and its mechanism in the functions of the mind.

The Freudian view of the make-up of the unconscious mind, which has worldwide acceptance, indicates that the mind as a whole consists of three main divisions. Our awareness, the part with which we think and reason, which is relatively small in comparison with the other parts, he called the *ego*, or conscious mind. Another part, best thought of as the conscience, he termed the *super-ego*. Below the consciousness is a part that he called the *id*, the largest phase of the psyche, this being the seat of memory, our basic instincts, our innate biological drives, our emotions, and suppressed desires. Later Freud theorized a fourth part lying between the id and the ego, just below the level of consciousness, calling it the *preconscious*. This part of the total mind is the basis of ordinary memory and operates in conjunction with the conscious.

For Freud, the ego is an area or part of the psychic structure that contrasts with the id. He considered it to be equivalent to consciousness, whose functions are the testing of reality; and it supports the external real world through the sense organs. Freud has compared it with the rider who "must curb the superior strength of his horse and must borrow the means to do so." The preconscious may be brought to consciousness without resistance. In other words, material recorded in the preconscious while not currently conscious is freely accessible to consciousness. Material in the unconscious is not. Contrary to the public usage by psychologists who use the term "subconscious" as a synonym for the unconscious, the term subconscious can be used synonymously with preconscious.

The unconscious part of the mind has certain dynamic qualities (not merely latent thoughts). It is the reservoir of inherent knowledge. It possesses intuitive power, is the residence of inspiration, invention, and genius.[1] When an idea is upsetting to a person it is usually forced into the unconscious and kept there by a process called repression. Such repressed ideas do not reach consciousness in spite of their effectiveness and intensity, and can be activated only with difficulty and against inner resistance. The unconscious mind is the source of our energy. No amount of will power exerted by the conscious mind can override it. The unconscious mind is uncritical, it accepts as absolute truth any idea allowed to enter its computer-like system. That is why, in children, because their conscious mind (critical sensor or critical factor) is not developed fully, the new ideas enter into their unconscious mind and become an integral part of their belief system and their consequent behavior.

The conscious mind of the adult, being critical, rejects some ideas and does not allow them to enter into the unconscious mind. The function of the conscious mind is to evaluate and compare each new idea it receives with previously accepted ideas and in this manner decide upon their veracity before accepting them in the unconscious memory bank. But the unconscious mind is incapable of discrimination and it believes anything it is told. If it could be made to believe that the person would die on a certain date he would surely do so. For this reason, it can be said that unconscious beliefs can cure or kill a person.[2] The unconscious mind is sometimes used synonomously with id.

Super-ego, conscience (or social aspect), contains the person's internalized ideas of right and wrong as taught by his parents. Super-ego is that part of the mental apparatus which criticizes the ego, and which produces distress, anxiety, or punishment whenever the ego extends to accept impulses emanating from the reservoir of primitive instinctual impulses (the id).

Both the id and super-ego are irrational systems in the sense that they completely ignore external reality. It is the function of the ego to mediate between the often conflicting demands of these two psychic forces and the real world and work out compromise behaviors acceptable to all three. If the ego is strong enough to curb the id and the gratification of its desires (defense mechanism), the person stays mentally healthy. If the ego is overpowered and resorts to extreme behavior it becomes a problem for the person, who is said to be mentally ill.

Freud believed the total unconscious mind to be composed of: id, preconscious, and the super-ego. It can be said that the total person is a unit composed of body and mind. The mind itself being composed of two main parts: the conscious and unconscious, each influencing the other. A comparison has been made by LeCron that the mind is like an iceberg floating in the sea. The conscious part is that above the water, about one-fifth of the iceberg. The unconscious is below the water and is about four-fifths of the total.[3]

The unconscious part of the mind not only acts through the autonomic nervous system but also undoubtedly controls it either by inhibition or by excitation. The unconscious mind controls the various functions of the body outside of consciousness, all the semi-voluntary and involuntary actions of the organs, glands, and muscles.

Another way the unconscious functions is at times to punish us (masochism) when guilt feelings are developed due to some transgression. Strangely, and showing something of its lack of logic, one part of the unconscious may lead us to "sin" or to do something wrong which we regret. Then another part, the conscious, goes to work and slaps us down for having done it.

Having studied the mechanism of this psychic triangle, we have to consider that when we are awake the conscious mind controls our actions, or most of them. Those organs and parts of the body which we can control by the exercise of will, or volition, are under the jurisdiction of the conscious mind.

When we are asleep, we are largely unconscious—the conscious part of the mind is subdued or inactive. Any movements or actions that we perform while asleep are caused by the unconscious mind; dreams are also initiated by unconscious activity. But during natural sleep, both the conscious and unconscious minds are inaccessible from the outside. They are asleep, though not totally.

An interesting aspect of hypnotic nature is the reverse

position of the conscious and unconscious mind. We know that in the ordinary state of the mind the conscious part is active in the foreground, and the unconscious part active in the background. But in hypnosis, this position is reversed. The result is that the conscious and unconscious minds are combined and the unconscious mind becomes dominant. We always do what our unconscious believes, even though we consciously know it is absurd. In hypnosis the conscious mind is bypassed temporarily so that our reasoning from a false idea can be stopped, and a correct premise substituted for the false one in the unconsciousness. Because under hypnosis the conscious mind is inhibited the truth can go directly to the unconscious without conscious censorship resulting from unconscious feedback. Granted that the unconscious mind will believe anything it is told we can re-program it. We can put aside the conscious mind and substitute new, constructive ideas for its existing negative ones. Of course, the conscious mind has the ability to reason and to make the most advantageous decision for the self, but its decision cannot be carried out unless the unconscious mind agrees to implement it. That is why we cannot take any step toward our behavior modification unless our unconscious mind is changed and agrees with our conscious mind to perform a new behavior. Therefore, our past habits and behaviors continue to dominate, and our will power can only hang on the surface until the unconscious mind is programmed for a new behavior. Then the new ideas that the unconscious mind has accepted must be reinforced daily until they become entrenched habits of thinking—influencing our behavior.[4]

The unconscious mind accepts only what the conscious mind accepts at the time the suggestion is given to the person. But if the conscious mind changes an idea or behavior after it has become entrenched in the unconscious mind, the unconsciousness will not change with it, rather the unconscious mind should again be approached and be made to accept the new idea or behavior.[5] Furthermore, under hypnosis the unconscious mind controls the entire organism, not only the voluntary nervous system, but also the involuntary nervous system. It is for this reason that mental and nervous disorders can be cured through hypnosis.[6]

Sidis contended that in hypnosis the two parts of the mind were dissociated, with the conscious mind inhibited and the unconscious mind open to suggestion.[7] He believed that dissociation begins with light hypnosis, and it is completed when a deep trance is reached.[8]

However, LeCron believes that in hypnosis the two sections of the mind cannot be regarded as having changed in any way since consciousness is retained, though the power to reason and think is restricted unless there is a stimulus for it to act. Suggestion can remove the hitch, and questioning serves as a stimulus. When questioned the subject is able to think, to compute, and to reason; and events that normally are impossible to recall can then be brought out. Except for memory recall and probably reasoning either the conscious or the unconscious mind can accomplish these functions. Everything that ever happened to us is stored in the memory in complete detail, and hypnosis can bring out forgotten memories even back to infancy.[9]

In short, hypnotic influence over the subject is based on the ability to reach the unconscious more directly in hypnosis. But how this happens, no one has yet discovered.[10]

REFERENCES

1. Winbigler, C. F., *Suggestion: Its Laws and Application* (New York: Psychology Publishing Co., 1928), p. 246.
2. Tebbetts, *Self-Hypnosis and Other Mind Expanding Techniques,* p. 11.
3. LeCron, L. M., *Self-Hypnotism: The Technique and Its Use in Daily Living* (New York: New American Library, 1964), p. 28.
4. Tebbetts, *Self-Hypnosis and Other Mind Expanding Techniques,* pp. 6-7.
5. *Ibid.,* p. 5.
6. LeCron and Bordeaux, *Hypnotism Today,* p. 145.
7. Sidis, B., *The Psychology of Suggestion* (New York: Arno Press, 1973), p. 69.
8. *Ibid.,* p. 69.
9. LeCron and Bordeaux, *Hypnotism Today,* p. 115.
10. *Ibid.,* p. 151.

CHAPTER SEVEN

QUALIFICATIONS OF THE HYPNOTIST

Hypnosis usually occurs after the hypnotist convinces his subject that he is able to refashion his mentality, alter his physiological status, and guide his behavior into a new and better mode. This requires the hypnotist to be a person of highest integrity, of empathetic attitude, knowledgeable, assertive, and pleasant in his manner. He also should be able to enlist the confidence and faith of the subject and attract his personality. Moreover, the hypnotist should be confident and master of his craft, and must look at the occurrence of hypnosis as an inevitability not a possibility. This trait, of course, does not mean that the hypnotist should have the Messiah Complex.* He should know his own personality characteristics, be fairly well-adjusted, and patient enough to consume as much time as necessary for the induction of hypnosis.

The hypnotist should always recognize his limits and by

---

*Overestimation of one's ability or power in a certain profession and being overconfident in oneself which usually leads to failure.

no means should he extend his activities beyond his professional knowledge or his technical capability. He should understand the critical impact of hypnosis and appreciate the fact that every hypnotic suggestion may affect the health and well-being of the subject. An experienced hypnotist should know the limitations of hypnosis and avoid the harms of an inappropriate or ill-advised suggestion so he never impedes the subject's physical capacity or normal body functions. A hypnotist who is not trained in hypnotherapy and behavior modification techniques should never experiment with hypnotherapy or give therapeutic suggestions to his subjects.

Since hypnosis is a part of psychology, a good hypnotist must have a good command of psychology. By using the principles of psychology, the hypnotist can take advantage of his subject's psychological characteristics during trance induction, to control the hypnotic process and secure the good of his subject. When a hypnotist administers hypnosis, he should focus on how to help the subject, not on how to increase his own power or prestige in the eyes of the subject or others.

The overall behavior and personality manifestations of the hypnotist should be gentle and respectful. The hypnotist should keep in his mind that the mere utterance of an inappropriate word or an irrelevant gesture may elicit the hatred of the subject and break his rapport.

Freud once stated that hypnosis gives the hypnotist more authority and respect than a priest or a "miracle man" could ever enjoy. This fact requires the hypnotist to possess outstanding characteristics and an extraordinary personality.

In summary, it is sufficient to refer to the biblical "golden rule"[1] and state that the hypnotist should do to the subject as he would have a hypnotist do to him.

REFERENCES

1. *The Holy Bible,* Luke 6:31, Matthew 7:12.

CHAPTER EIGHT

CONDITIONS OF THE HYPNOTIC ENVIRONMENT

Conditions in the immediate place of induction such as temperature, light, color, sound, and odor have a great influence on the induction of hypnosis and should be suitable for this purpose. The emotional and physical condition of the subject is also of great significance in induction and should be checked.

Temperature—even temperature, probably between 73 and 75 degrees Fahrenheit, somewhat on the warm side, is suitable for bodily comfort during induction. A sudden draft of air can hinder induction and may even result in waking a subject who has already been hypnotized. When a person is hypnotized, if the place is a little too warm or a little too cool, the temperature can be modified by suggestion.

Light—It is best that lighting be subdued and no light should shine into the eyes of the subject. If it is daytime, shades should be drawn in order to produce a subdued effect. At night a single lamp may be placed behind the subject. Indirect lighting is always preferable.

Colors—The right colors can produce a very favorable

effect for the induction of hypnosis. According to Arons it has been found that blues and greens, due to their restful and soothing effect, are the best colors for the induction of hypnosis. Anything in the red family seems to be tiring and irritating; orange and yellow colors are particularly unsuitable.[1]

Noise—A quiet place helps the induction process. Discordant noises should be avoided. If subdued noise is employed in the background as though it emanated from a closet or adjoining room, it can have a calming and relaxing effect and help the induction of hypnosis.

Odors—Unpleasant odors such as those of garlic, onion, trash, etc. are detrimental to the induction of hypnosis. Because of hypersensitivity, which is one of the characteristics of hypnosis, even a person who is tolerant of some odors such as tobacco in his waking state, may find them irritating under hypnosis (to the extent that he may be awakened). On the other hand, certain sweet odors are helpful for the induction of hypnosis.

Climate—Climate seems to have an effective role in the production of hypnosis. It has been said that hypnotic induction is much easier in warm countries than in cold ones, probably because the natives of these countries are accustomed to relaxation.[2] Therefore the French should be more susceptible to hypnosis than the Scandinavians and Germans. In the tropics hypnosis is said to appear rapidly and become very deep.[3]

The physical condition of the subject—The subject should be put at ease and his overall comfort must be assured for induction. He may either lie on a couch or sit in an easy chair completely relaxed. When sitting in a chair both of his feet should be flat on the floor with legs extended, hands resting on the arms of the chair or in his lap. A reclining chair which will tip back and has a footrest is ideal for induction, because the subject may choose either to sit up or lie back at any angle according to his preference. The greatest relaxation is gained by having the subject lie down on a couch in the normal position of sleep. Knees and ankles must never be crossed. The mere weight of the hands or arms on the chest or abdomen may retard the induction process.

Restrictive clothing such as ties, collars, and belts should be loosened and shoes must be removed if not comfortable. In the case of female subjects particular attention should be paid to their corsets and shoes. Naturally, a full bladder would be a hindrance to induction.

If the subject suffers from pain or any kind of physical discomfort, the induction of hypnosis may fail. However, the presence of a severe pain may become an incentive for a person to seek relief in hypnosis and, as a result, will go quickly into trance. Subjects with a severe cough or a cold should not be induced for the first time, as they often are disturbed by coughing, sneezing, or the need to clear their throats. Others may have a postnasal drip, and this can be a distinct hindrance to induction.

Overtiredness may lead to failure of induction. If a person is physically exhausted, he may go into a natural sleep rather than into trance. The more normal the condition of a subject, the easier he goes under a trance.

Drugs and alcoholic beverages—As a rule, when a person's mind is clouded or the higher centers of the brain are dull, the ability to concentrate will diminish and therefore the induction of hypnosis becomes difficult if not impossible. For this reason an intoxicated subject can't be easily hypnotized because intoxication impairs his ability to concentrate.

However, pertinent experiments show that a minor dosage of a drug can be used as a "placebo" and probably helps the induction of hypnosis. The reason is not clear. Perhaps it is because, as Wolberg suggested, hypnosis and drugs partially act upon the same cortical loci,[4] or possibly drugs lay the ground for dissociation of awareness.[5] Whatever the cause might be, narcotics of all sorts can seemingly help in production of hypnosis if given in proper dosage because they develop symptoms of sleep. However, drugs do not directly produce hypnorelaxation, but they can increase the effectiveness of waking suggestibility. It should also be borne in mind that too small a dose does not sufficiently affect the subject's suggestibility, wheras too large a dose will depress him too much. Sometimes a "hypnotic pill" (an innocuous sugar pill) is administered, after the patient is first told that it is a potent drug for the induction of hypnosis. The success of this method with difficult subjects is not conclusive.

Alcoholic beverages also seem to have the same effect as narcotics in the production of hypnosis if the proper amount is used. Careful use of alcoholic beverages may be useful for the production of hypnosis. Provided the subject is still able to concentrate and pay attention, alcoholic drinks generally remove inhibition and release nervous tension and as a result make the hypnotic state easier to teach.

In brief, nowhere has it been shown conclusively that any drug or alcoholic beverage induces a hypnotic state by itself. The exact action of drugs and alcoholic beverages are far from clear. Therefore these items, even tranquilizers, should be avoided in the induction of hypnosis.

Emotions—Different kinds of emotions can have favorable as well as unfavorable effects upon the induction of hypnosis. Love, respect, trust, goodwill, and sympathy for the operator, and his reputation in the eyes of the subject are favorable factors for the induction of hypnosis. While anger, fear, irritation, distrust, hate and animosity are, conversely, unfavorable elements.

Audience—If the hypnotic process is being performed in the presence of an audience, the hypnotist should be careful not to permit any member of the audience to interfere with the hypnotic process. Sometimes in the middle of the induction a bystander may laugh or giggle and this will interrupt the concentration of the subject and may lead to the failure of the process.

REFERENCES

1. Arons, *New Master Course in Hypnotism,* p. 56.
2. *Ibid.,* p. 53.
3. Friedrich Bjornstorm, *Hypnotism: Its History and Present Development,* trans. Baron Nils Posse (New York: Humboldt Library, No. 113), p. 12.
4. Wolberg, *Medical Hypnosis,* 1: 144.
5. Weitzenhoffer, *General Techniques of Hypnotism,* p. 256.

CHAPTER NINE

SUGGESTIBILITY TESTS

Suggestibility tests or waking suggestions are used to evaluate the degree of hypnotizability and succeptibility* of subjects to suggestions. Waking suggestions determine how fast people respond to hypnosis and are the basic rules employed to predict the probable outcome of any attempt to use hypnosis on an individual.

Broadly speaking, the methods used for inducing hypnosis and waking suggestions may be divided into two general categories: direct or authoritarian types and indirect or permissive types. The direct or authoritarian types denote a strong, commanding, dominating approach. The indirect or permissive types are soft spoken, persuasive, convincing and easy-going. With the authoritarian type of induction, the tone is louder and the words are spoken more rapidly and forcefully. With the permissive type of induction the voice is kept low and the subject almost coaxed into the trance.

---

*The term suggestibility or trance capacity refers to the natural ability of a subject to be hypnotized, and the term hypnotizability involves the net effect of suggestibility plus any operative situational factors affecting the hypnotic ability of a subject at a given time.[1]

The type of technique employed will depend on the personality of the subject. The authoritarian approach will work better with permissive and also nervous people, while the permissive approach may suit submissive people. Consideration of the subjects's psychological background, with all his feelings, ideas, and attitudes, allow the hypnotist to decide what he wishes—not what the hypnotist desires. Nonetheless an extremely authoritarian type of induction is seldom as effective as the permissive approach. Psychological evaluation of the subject helps the hypnotist to decide which one of these methods should be chosen to obtain more effective results.

Psychological tests are used by a professional hypnotist, only when he intends to condition a person to accept hypnosis, teaching self-hypnosis, or when he is demonstrating stage hypnosis. More will be explained about this aspect of induction, when "Methods of Induction" are discussed.

Fross has an interesting idea about hypnotizability tests. He states that he does not use any test for hypnotizability, on the assumption that all subjects are good until proved otherwise. He reasons that if a subject fails to pass one or two tests, it may have a negative effect on him and make the induction more difficult.[2] Moreover, granted that the best subject cannot be hypnotized unless he wants to be, hypnotic suggestibility tests are valid only when the subject is well motivated and cooperates with the trance induction procedure.

There are many suggestibility tests, the most significant of them are outlined below:

(1) Chevreul's Pendulum Test

This is one of the oldest and most popular tests of hypnotizability. It is named after Chevreul, a French chemist who, in 1812 initiated it. Chevreul in his studies found out that the subjects thought was the sole cause of Pendulum's movement. This thought acted through the intervention of imperceptible movements, which were involuntary and unconscious. Two centuries later, William James postulated that any idea, unless inhibited, tended to express itself automatically in behavior. Today this phenomenon is termed "ideomotor activity," or the involuntary capacity of muscles to respond to thoughts, feelings, and ideas.

The Chevreul Pendulum is made of a strong thread or a chain about 8 to 10 inches long, attached to a heavy ring, key, or a glass ball, preferably bright and shiny. Next a heavy circle eight inches in diameter is drawn on a white paper or cardboard. Inside the circle two heavy lines are drawn crossing each other at the center. The vertical line may be designated as A—B, the horizontal line as C—D, and the center as X.

Now the subject sits at a table, rests his left forearm near the edge of the table, rests his right elbow with his right arm a little forward of his left arm holding the end of the thread between his finger tips. He should adjust his position to be comfortable. See figure 1. The subject may also stand upright, feet together, with the body relaxed. In the standing position his elbow must not touch his sides, and the chart is placed on a chair or low table. The subject is told not to make any conscious effort to move or hinder the movements of the ball, because the ball will move spontaneously by just thinking about it. He is told that the mere concentration upon the movement of the ball from left to right, forward or backward, clockwise or counterclockwise, will cause it to swing in accordance with his thoughts. It is sug-

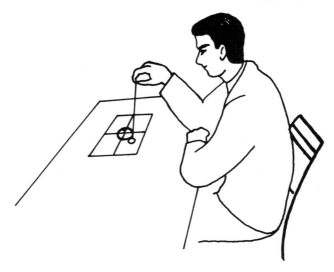

Figure 1

gested to the subject that he will be unable to control the swing of the ball. Continuous strong suggestion is then given to the effect that the ball is beginning to swing ... back and forth ... right to left ... clockwise ... or counterclockwise, and that the swing is increasing etc.

The actual swing of the pendulum in inches constitutes the score on this test. Extremely susceptible individuals react in full accordance with the suggestions.

(2) Arms Rising and Falling Test

In this test the hypnotist asks the subject to stand upright in a relaxed position, with his feet together and his arms loosely at his sides. Then he is given the following suggestions:

"Close your eyes and listen effortlessly to the sound of

my voice. This is a test of the power of your mind over your body and shows how well you can use your imagination. Stretch your arms out at shoulder level, your left palm facing the ceiling and your extended right thumb also pointing to the ceiling.

Now, imagine that your right thumb is tied with a cord and that this cord extends up into the air and is attached to a balloon and a heavy dictionary is put on your upturned left palm. Imagine that the balloon is pulling your right arm and the dictionary is pushing the left arm down. Imagine your right arm is getting lighter and lighter and rising in the air — your left arm is getting heavier and heavier and falling down. Right arm going up — left arm going down. Right arm getting lighter, left arm getting heavier." See Figure 2. This suggestion will continue by the hypnotist for several minutes.

Figure 2

Then the subject would be told to open his eyes and watch the position of his hands. Good, responsive subjects will notice that unconsciously the position of their arms and their body have changed. This is a permissive test and no commanding or authoritative tone is administered in the suggestions. This test can be applied individually or with groups.

(3) The Hand Clasp Test

Before starting this test, the subject should be requested to remove any ring he may be wearing, otherwise he may bruise his fingers. The subject can be either in a standing or a sitting position. See Figure 3. When in a standing position, he is asked to stretch out his arms either in front of him at eye level, or above his head, clasp his hands gently, and interlock his finger, but not to squeeze them tightly together. Another variant of the standing position is that the subject

Figure 3

bends his arms at the elbows. See figure 4. If in the sitting position, the subject rests his clasped hands on his lap. Before beginning, the hypnotist clasps his own hands in the desired manner, explaining to the subject where his hands should be placed. Then he takes hold of the subjects hands and squeezes them gently together. Asking him to look into his eyes or to close his eyes or to keep his eyes on his own hands and to watch the reactions to follow, the hypnotist says the following directly and authoritatively in a commanding fashion. "Lock your hands tightly together — tighter and tighter. Your fingers are locking together more and more. Your hands and fingers are sticking together more and more. Imagine that you can not unclasp your hands. Your hands and your fingers are so glued together that you are unable to tell the left from the right and the right from the left. Your hands are stuck fast, you can not take them apart. I am going to count to

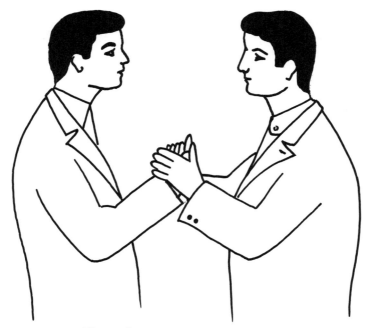

Figure 4

three. With each number that I count, and with each breath that you take, you find your fingers sticking tighter and tighter together. When I reach the count of "three" your fingers are so completely locked together, your hands are so completely stuck together that you can not pull them apart. Now ... one ... two ... three... You can not open your hands. Try but you can not. Now stop trying."

For the best results, the hypnotist, keeps fixating the subject throughout, and he gives the suggestions in rapid succession while the subject tries to meet the challenge.

When this test is successful, it indicates a high degree of suggestibility. If the test fails, the hypnotist says: "That was difficult, wasn't it?" Then he explains to the subject that a person may unconsciously refuse to cooperate with one approach but be very cooperative with another. He immediately employs another method, until a satisfactory result is obtained.

There are variations of this test, one of which is to have the subject place his hands over his head with the fingers interlocked and the palms facing outward. Naturally, with some subjects, a permissive approach is preferable.

(4) The Backward Postural Sway Test

The subject is asked to stand in a relaxed position with his heels and toes together, his hands at his sides, his eyes closed, and tilt his head slightly up and back. The hypnotist stands about one foot behind the subject and places the palms of his hands against the subject's shoulder blades. The operator's hands should be so placed that the tips of his fingers hook over the subject's shoulders in order to be able to pull the subject gently backwards. Then he tells the subject that as he pulls his hands back from the subject's shoulders, he will feel a force pulling him backward. To dispel any fears of falling back on the floor, the hypnotist instructs the subject to fall back and even may pull him back gently to assure him that the hypnotist is standing behind him and will catch him. Thereafter the hypnotist pulls his hands away very gently and slowly and says:

"You are falling back, falling back, back, back into my hands. I will catch you. Something like a magnetic power is pulling you back. You are beginning to lose your balance. Let yourself go. You are falling. The more you resist the force of the magnetic power which is pulling you back, the harder it will be to remain standing still. You feel it pulling and you are letting yourself go back. Falling . . . falling . . .back . . .backward . . .backward . . .falling . . . . back . . .back . . .back . . . " . (See Figure 5)

A good subject will fall backwards without any difficulty. There are a series of variations of this test. One variation is that the hypnotist rests his hands slightly on the subject's shoulders and pulls him gently but firmly backwards. The remainder of the procedure is much the same as before, except that the hypnotist, after introductory instructions, will say: "In a few minutes I will ask you to think of falling backward into my hands."

Still another variation of this test which is particularly valuable for resistant subjects is that the hypnotist stands directly behind the subject and extends his arms, with his fingertips in front of the subject's face. While mention of falling backwards is made, the hypnotist's hands are moved forward slowly, producing the illusion in the subject that he is actually falling back.

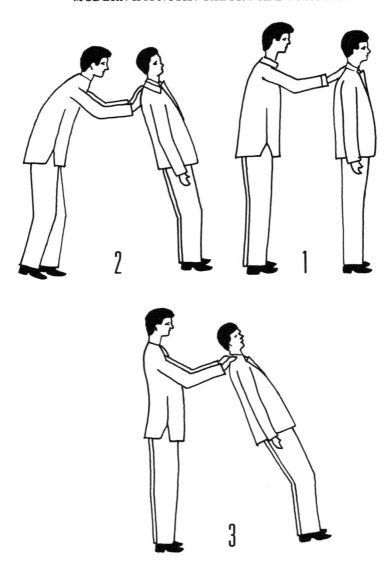

Figure 5

(5) The Forward Postural Sway Test

This test is a variation of the backward postural sway test. The hypnotist stands in front of the subject—quite close to him. Leaning forward so that his face approaches the subject's, he states the following: "I want you to look into my eyes." At this point the hypnotist gazes on the bridge of the subject's nose, and raises his elbows horizontally, bringing the tips of his extended hands to either side of the subject's head so as almost to touch the temples. The hypnotist's elbows are in a flexed position (See Figure 6). The verbalization is the same as in the previous experiment, except that the word "forward" is used instead of the word "backward."

In all of the waking suggestions the experienced hypnotist tells his subjects that not only will they be unable to resist the suggested actions, but that the more they try to resist, the less they will be able to do so.

(6) The Eyeball Test

The subject is asked to keep his eyelids closed, to roll up his eyeballs, and to look upward at a point indicated by the hypnotist (by touching the forehead). The hypnotist then states the following:

"Keep your eyes closed. Your lids are sticking tightly together. Keep your eyeballs upward. Look up...up... Your eyelids are glued tightly together. They are stuck fast. The muscles of your eyes are so flaccid that they cannot move. It seems that you have lost the control of the muscles that open and close your eyes. You cannot and will not be able to open them. No matter how hard you try, you cannot

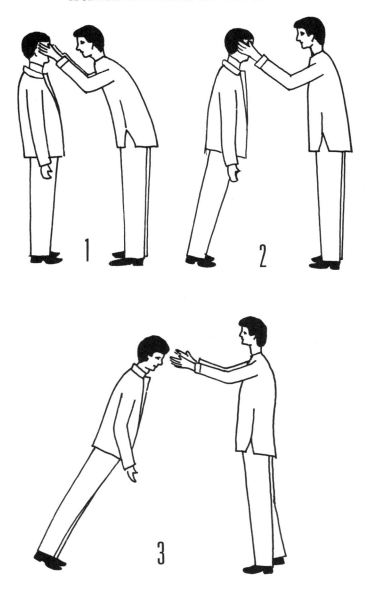

Figure 6

open them. Now try to open them. You cannot! You cannot open them. Stop trying and relax. From this moment you will be able to open your eyes whenever you choose.

This test is actually based upon physiological factors rather than psychological ones. The subject does not realize that it is extremely difficult to open the lids when the eyeballs are rolled up into the head. Naturally the eyeballs must come down before the eyelids can be opened. The subject thinks that the effect is due to the hypnotist's suggestions. If the individual is unable to open his eyes, he can be considered a good subject.

(7) The Hand Levitation Test

This test can be used for evaluating the subject's susceptibility to hypnosis and also as part of the induction method. The hand levitation method for the induction of hypnosis, rather a difficult one, was initiated by Erickson. The best description of it is given by Wolberg. This method is used indirectly and permissively: The subject is told to sit comfortably in a chair and place his hands in his lap. Then the hypnotist says the following:

"Would you mind focusing on your left hand (the one which is closer to the hypnotist). While you are focusing on your left hand effortlessly, you will soon feel some kind of sensation in it. Perhaps at first it may be a prickly sensation, or a numb feeling, or perhaps one of your fingers will begin to move or separate. Or perhaps one of the fingers may begin to twitch. Concentrate on your hand and you will gradually begin to feel it losing its weight and becoming lighter and lighter. You will feel your hand floating, and it will begin to rise up into the air. As your hand and your fingers begin to lift, your arm will also get lighter and lighter—so light that you can feel it going up, going up, rising, and you cannot hold it down. It feels so good, so light, so very light . . . Still rising higher and higher . . . Let it go now, faster and easier. Your hand is moving up toward your face. You can decide what part of your face you want your hand to touch. The moment it touches your face, you will let yourself go into a deep refreshing sleep. Now your hand is getting very close to your face. Soon it will touch your face and when it does, your eyelids will close, and you will drift away into sleep . . . a delightful, soothing sleep. "

If the hand and arm are raised and touch the face of the subject, he can be considered an excellent subject . In this case, the induction into deeper hypnosis should take place.

Experienced hypnotists do not completely depend upon suggestibility tests. The subjects may respond positively to these tests, but still they may not enter the hypnotic state. Nonetheless, if the subjects do not respond positively to suggestibility tests, it is indicative of negative suggestibility. Most of these tests are not valid, because hypnosis is dependent upon many factors such as belief, confidence, expectation and the like, while these tests are based upon ideomotor and ideosensory activities.

Moreover, they do not show which kind of method should be applied to hypnotize the subject effectively. Here the advantage of Fross's idea will be realized. Many subjects might have been hypnotized readily without the suggestibility tests; whereas application of these tests may interfere with rapport and render the hypnotic process abortive.

REFERENCES

1. Udolf, *Handbook of Hypnosis for Professionals,* p. 31.
2. Fross, G. H., *Handbook of Hypnotic Techniques* (S. Orange, NJ.: Power Publishers, 1979), p. 26.

CHAPTER TEN

INDUCTION OF HYPNOSIS

The induction of hypnosis can be divided into three stages: the preparation of the subject, the actual induction and the deepening of the trance. Because of the significance of these topics, each of them will be examined in a separate chapter.

Preparation of the subject consists of the pre-induction talk and selection of the method. This may or may not include various tests of suggestibility. The successful completion of this stage enables the hypnotist to establish rapport with the subject.

In the actual induction stage, specific trance inducing techniques are employed to bring about the hypnotic state. In the trance deepening stage which usually merges imperceptibly with the actual induction stage, various techniques are used.

Preparation of the Subject

Pre-Induction Talk—Before the induction of hypnosis, the hypnotist should try to obtain from the subject a picture of his psychological make up, his idea, and his feelings. This helps the hypnotist to choose an appropriate method for induction and prepares the subject for undergoing hypnosis. This is called the pre-induction talk. The pre-induction talk is particuarly helpful with the skeptical or apprehensive subject who is either ignorant of the nature of hypnosis or has some misconceptions about it.

The hypnotist explains the nature of hypnosis, that hypnosis is a healthful and restful experience, that there are untold advantages to its use, and that no possible harm can result from its practice. The hypnotist also explains that attainment of hypnosis is not a mental tug of war and that it will be obtained only through the cooperation of the subject by following the suggestions of the hypnotist; that the capacity to be hypnotized is within the subject, and the hypnotist merely brings it to the surface acting only as a guide. It should also be emphasized that no one can be hypnotized against his will; that the subject even in deep hypnosis will do nothing to violate his moral code; that he will not reveal information of a personal nature, unless he wishes to do so; that he will be completely in control of himself, aware of his environment; that at no time will he lose his consciousness under hypnosis; and that he will not act contrary to his wishes. The hypnotist explains what he is going to do, what is expected of the subject, all the signs or symptoms of approaching hypnotic relaxation, and all the pleasant feelings that the subject will experience under hypnosis.

As a result of this preparatory consultation, the hypnotist can eliminate the fear, anxiety, apprehension, and tension that are naturally present in all individuals undergoing hypnotic induction for the first time. During this initial interview the hypnotis gathers—for hypnotic purposes—the relevant facts about the psychological character, life experiences, and education of the subject. At the end of the pre-induction talk, the hypnotist should ask the subject whether he has any questions that concern him about the nature of hypnosis.

The pre-induction talk enables the hypnotist to fit his method of induction to the individual subject's needs and character. In selecting the form of induction to be used the decision should rest on the observations that the hypnotist makes about the subject. It would be a mistake to adopt a forceful, commanding technique with one who is authoritative and aggressive in his character, and vice versa. With the permissive approach the hypnotist tries to secure the cooperation of the subject by avoiding any procedure, patter, gesture, and cadence that builds up anxiety in the subject. The subject is led to understand that the hypnotic state can be reached only through his own cooperation.

With the authoritative approach the hypnotist takes full control of the hypnotic induction and dominates the subject. The subject is made to believe that he must comply totally with the demands of the hypnotist. The subject is also told that if the hypnotist tells him that hypnotic phenomena will occur, it will definitely do so and that he has no choice but to accept its occurance and finally the trance state.

The pre-induction talk helps to increase the hypnotist's prestige and good rapport will be established between the hypnotist and the subject, thus ensuring successful hypnosis.

Selection of Method

Pre-induction talk gives a good opportunity to the hypnotist to select an appropriate method to hypnotize the subject effectively. There are as many techniques of induction as there are hypnotists. No one technique is superior to any other, but there is always at least one technique which is better suited for a given setting and a given subject. A skilful hypnotist knows how and when to choose the right technique. It is also possible that more than one technique may be needed for the same individual at different times.

Sometimes a method which seems to be completely inappropriate may be capable of causing a deeper trance than one which appears more effective to the hypnotist. The minds and emotional qualities of people differ. A successful technique may lead to failure when the hypnotist has ignored the possible predjudice of the subject against the process. Each subject will have a natural, purely individualistic orientation which will lead him to accept one method and reject another one. A university professor will easily respond to a method which seems scientifically admissible to him, but that same method may fail with a prejudiced individual.

As a whole, the technique used must fit the needs of the subject at that particular time, taking into account his personality and his belief system. A most important factor is the interpersonal relationship between the hypnotist and the subject (rapport). In most cases, failure is the result of the hypnotist attempting to adjust the subject to the method, rather than adjusting the method to the subject.

CHAPTER ELEVEN

ACTUAL INDUCTION

In view of the fact that nearly all modern techniques combine visual fixation (objective approach) with suggestion (subjective approach) it is worthwhile to examine their combined use.

The induction process may range from instructions to the subject to close his eyes and imagine a restful scene (subjective method), to making him stare at a spot in his hand or a shining object (objective method), until his eyes become tired and closed, the purpose being to divert the subject's attention from his general environment and focus it on a particular spot. At the same time he is encouraged to relax. This enables him to become receptive to the hypnotic state, because whenever a person relaxes, he concentrates more completely and becomes more open to new ideas.

To put it simply, to induce hypnosis, the hypnotist will begin by directing the subject to follow four general rules: to relax his body, to make his mind inactive, to fix his attention on an object and to listen to the sound of the hypnotist's voice. The subject may close his eyes and mentally focus his attention on an object. Although this method is desirable for eliminating distractions, it is not mandatory. The author prefers his subjects to keep their eyes open during the actual induction. He can then watch the movements of the subject's eyes and follow the progress of hypnosis, until the eyelids involuntarily close.

There are many variations of the eye fixation method. The subject may be asked to gaze into the eyes of the hypnotist or to direct his attention to some object. Hull believes that gazing into the eyes of the hypnotist leads to quicker results. In this method, the hypnotist brings his own eyes within eight inches of those of the subject. The subject should then be asked to focus on one of the eyes of the hypnotist. Should the subject feel uneasy about gazing into the hypnotist's eyes, he can gaze at some object, preferably a bright one. This can be almost anything as long as no discomfort is caused by staring at it. A Chevreul pendulum, a silver Christmas tree ornament, a picture on the wall, a spot, a crack on the wall or ceiling, a doorknob, or a thumb-tack stuck in the end of a pencil are just some of the many possibilities. In some cases the subject is asked to fix his attention on the tip or bridge of his or the hypnotist's nose, or to imagine a spot on the center of his own forehead and to fix his attention on it.

If a small fixation object such as a crystal ball is used, it should be held about eight inches or so, from the subject's eyes and slightly above his eye level. Larger objects should be placed at proportionately greater distances from the subject's eyes.

Many gadgets or so called "hypno-aids" are available and may be used for induction. The most popular of such gadgets are: hour glasses, hypnotrones, hypnoscopes, hypnodisks, whirling spirals, and metronomes.

Another technique to tire the eyes of the subject is to ask him to open and close his eyes as the hypnotist counts backwards from one hundred. The subject is instructed to open his eyes on the even numbers and to close them on the odd ones. From a slow beginning, the hypnotist accelerates the rate of counting, then slows down again. If the subject has difficulty in following this technique the procedure is ended. (psychic method).

It should be carefully noted that in visual fixation the purpose is effortless concentration of attention upon an idea or an object rather than visual fixation with conscious effort.

When the subject has complied with the four rules mentioned above (relaxation of the body, inactiveness of the mind, fixation of attention on an object and listening to the hypnotist's voice) the hypnotist begins his induction talk. In its purest form, it consists of telling the subject over and over again in a progressive manner that he is going to sleep; that his eyes are heavy, tired, that they are closing, and that he is falling asleep; that indeed, he is fast asleep. (This method is called the verbal method).

If the hypnotist alludes to some physical changes in the subject which he does not feel, then the hypnotist will be discredited and the subject will tend to reject any suggestions which follow. If the hypnotist tells the subject that his eyes are getting tired, or that he feels drowsy, the subject should actually feel these bodily developments. The hypnotist may mention possible future sensations, but should not say, they are happening, until they actually occur.

Arons suggests that the introduction phase has three parts: the preparatory stage, when the hypnotist speaks in the future tense; the second stage, when the subject is feeling the symptoms of approaching hypnosis, (in this stage the hypnotist speaks in the present tense, in a gentle manner using a relatively monotonous low pitched voice); and the final stage, when there is enough evidence to believe that the subject is hypnotized and suggestions are given in a more direct, emphatic and authoritarian way. This stage actually covers the deepening stage too.[1]

These steps are used in most methods of induction. However, in instantaneous and very quick methods of inductions, the first two stages are usually eliminated.

Techniques of hypnotic induction which combine visual, auditory, and tactile elements may be more effective than techniques which use only one of these. Listening intently to falling rain, the drip of a leaky faucet, the steady hum of a motor, the click of a clock or a watch, the clicking wheels of a train—or anything that goes on continously in a monotonous way—can effect the senses and bring about hypnosis.

Patter in Hypnosis

In hypnosis, the term "patter" means the words and suggestions which are used to produce a condition of hypnosis. During induction, the hypnotist should to a great extent imitate a mother who sings a lullaby to her infant to induce sleep. As the hypnotist talks, his voice becomes progressively slower, softer and more monotonous. A slight musical tone is appropriate and harsh phrases must be avoided.

Words and phrases should be chosen for their quality. For instance, "more limp and more drowsy" are more soothing than "limper and drowsier." The "ier" sound seems to be slightly more harsh. Similarly "so-o-o sleepy" or "more and more sleepy" are better than "sleepier."

In giving suggestions, the hypnotist should talk to the subject at the level of his perception and the words and phrases should be so chosen and constructed as to be easily understood. The hypnotist should bear in mind that it is not what he says that is important but what the subject hears. A great deal of communication in everyday life as well as in hypnosis is carried out by implication or even recognized by the participants. We see this in everyday life when a housewife, for example, bangs her pots a bit louder when she is displeased with her husband but may hum softly to herself when she is pleased. She may not recognize what she is doing, and her husband may not always know quite how he is getting the message, but he feels it at some level.[2]

Time Factor

The induction of hypnosis for the average susceptible person coming to be hypnotized for the first time takes between three and twenty minutes. Later inductions require no more than three or five minutes or less.

Some hypnotists become impatient with new subjects who fail to respond readily and accuse them of a lack of concentration, spiteful resistance or unhypnotizability. These hypnotists, sometimes make it difficult for subsequent hypnotists to hypnotize the subjects with whom they have had failure. At the very least, this failure will destroy in the subject any belief or expectations they may have had in hypnosis. The author has many times encountered subjects who say they are unhypnotizable, because some hypnotists have already tried to hypnotize them and have failed to do so. To their surprise, I have found them susceptible to hypnosis. The reason for their earlier failure has most probably been the impatience or lack of time spent by hypnotists who previously worked on them.

Marcuse says: "In certain mental hospitals there were reports that anywhere up to 300 hours (not consecutive) were required before the patient could be considered hypnotized. In cases where a profound degree of hypnosis is needed for the resolution of complicated behaviour, eight hours of training of even initially susceptible subjects may be needed in order to obtain a satisfactory depth."[3] Erickson, who claims to have hypnotized over 3500 individuals sums up the situation well by stating that although one of his subjects had reached a profound trance on the first induction in less than 30 seconds, he had also had one who had required 300 hours of systematic work before the first signs of any trance were produced.[4] Erickson also pointed out that with difficult subjects, a deep sleep may come only after two, three, or even four hours of continued sleep suggestion.[5]

Most hypnotists agree that the longer the induction time the more likely it is that the subject will be hypnotized and the deeper will be the state achieved.

REFERENCES

1. Arons, *New Master Course in Hypnotism,* pp. 74-75.
2. Milton H. Erickson and Ernest L. Rossi, *Hypnotherapy: An Explanatory Casebook,* (New York: Halsted Press Divsion of John Wiley and Sons, Inc., 1979), p.38.
3. Marcuse, *Hypnosis: Fact and Fiction,* p.59.
4. Weitzenhoffer, *General Techniques of Hypnotism,* p.269.
5. Erickson, "The Application of Hypnosis to Psychiatry," *Medical Record,* 150:60, 1939.

CHAPTER TWELVE

METHODS OF INDUCTION OF HYPNOSIS

Induction methods and procedures are many and varied. Generally they can be divided into three groups: Objective* and physical (or physiological) methods, subjective or psychic methods and psychophysical methods.

Physical and Objective Methods

Those who use objective and physical (or physiological) methods for the induction of hypnosis, believe that hypnosis is a condition of the nervous system, resulting from sensory fatigue or induced nervous reactions from objective gadgets and physical devices such as strokings, passes, pressures, etc., which affect a portion of the brain. Proponents of this method maintain that by having the subject stare intently at

---

*All the methods which require the subject to gaze intently at an object in such a way that intense ocular fatigue is produced, are called the "fascination method." Some hypnotists use their own eyes as the object of fixation, others use a small shining object, or even a spot on the hand or on the wall.

an object, his eyes will be sufficiently strained so that with suggestions of sleep the hypnotic state is produced. They disregard suggestion by itself as a method for the production of hypnosis. The sacred principle of objectivists is: "Tire the senses of the subject and hypnotic sleep will follow."[1]

The most famous objectivists and their methods are outlined below:

Mesmer used physical as well as objective methods, and also a combination of them, for inducing hypnosis. He used to have groups of his patients sit around a large tub called a "baquet" filled with iron filings and bottles of water, and have them hold on to one of the many iron rods which protruded from the tub. If there were not enough iron rods for everyone to have their own, it did not matter, because the extra patients needed only place their arms on a person who was actually holding a rod, and the magnetism would supposedly flow through to them (objective method). Mesmer also would take the subject's hands in his own hands and stare into their eyes at the time of induction. Then he would release his grasp and would make passes over the subject's body (physico-objective method).

Passes were traditionally used by some hypnotists but they are now an outmoded method. Furthermore, they have no real value and are used as indirect suggestions.

Esdaile would direct his subject to lie on his back in bed. Then he would stand at the head of the bed, leaning directly over the subject, so that their eyes met in a steady stare at about 8 to 15 inches (objective method). Then with one hand he would press lightly on the subject's stomach; (See figure 7) with the other, he affected rhythmic strokings over the subject's eyes. He also blew gently on the subject's nose, on the eyeballs and between the lips (physical method).[2]

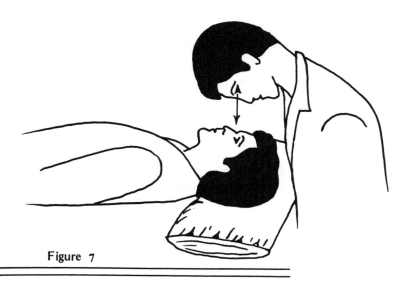

Figure 7

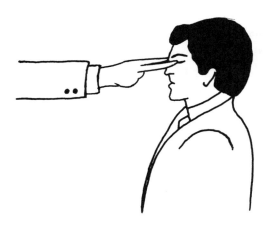

Figure 8

Braid's method, still a popular one, was that he would hold a small bright object about 8 to 15 inches from the subject (above eye level) to cause strain upon the subject's eyes. Later Braid found that it was not the visual fixation but the attendant concentration of attention which was responsible for hypnosis (objective or fascination method).

Liebeault would extend his hand and arm, forefinger and middle fingers forming a V, about two feet from the subject's forehead or eyebrows. At the same time, he would make suggestions to the patient, moving his fingers very close to the subject's eyes or even touching them. (See figure 8) This caused the subject's eyelids to droop and eventually close. Then a few suggestions of "sleep" would induce a hypnotic trance (physico-objective method).

Bernheim also used his index and middle fingers forming a V, but about 8 inches from the subject's eyes, only for the purpose of concentration of attention. (See figure 9) Of course, this technique was accompanied by appropriate suggestion (objective method).

Charcot used hearing, touch and the patient's sense of smell, in addition to the purely visual methods of trance induction. To make the subject drowsy he would produce a monotonous stimulation of the auditory sense. For example, he would place a motor close to the subject's ear, hoping that its constant, monotonous hum would bring about hypnosis. At times he would take advantage of the rhythmic beating of a hollow-sounding bell for the same purpose (objective method).

Psychic or Subjective Methods

Those who take advantage of subjective methods of

Figure 9

induction, depend upon the psyche. They believe that suggestion is the only causative factor in producing hypnosis. To them, physical devices are unimportant for the induction of hypnosis and they are used only as window dressing to misdirect the attention.

Gindes contends that it is not only gazing intently at some dazzling object or even being subjected to passes of the hypnotist which brings about sensory fatigue and produces hypnosis. He believed that by using subjective methods, which rely entirely on suggestion it is possible to create the desired state more effectively, more predictably, and with more practical results.[3]

Any statement made by the operator or any action which he applies will have the desired effect if the subject believes that it will; if he expects it to; and if he combines his belief and expectation with sufficient imagination for it to come about.

The most successful applications of subjective methods for the production of hypnosis were made by Liebeault and particularly Bernheim.* Bernheim, here describes his method:

"I proceed to hypnotize in the following manner: I begin by saying to the patient that I believe benefit is to be derived from the use of suggestive therapeutics, that it is possible to cure or relieve him by hypnotism; that there is nothing either hurtful or strange about it; that it is an ordinary sleep. . . . . and that this beneficial condition restores the equilibrium of the nervous system, etc. . . . . when I have thus banished from his mind the fear that attaches to the idea of magnetism and to that unknown condition. . . . . he gives himself up, then I say:

'Look at me and think of nothing but sleep. Your eyelids begin to feel heavy, your eyes tired. They begin to wink, they are getting moist, you cannot see distinctly. They are closed.' Some subjects close their eyes and are asleep immediately. With others, I have to repeat, lay more stress on what I say, and even make gestures. . . . . I hold two fingers of my right hand before the patient's eyes, or persuade him to fix his eyes upon mine, endeavoring at the same time to concentrate his attention upon the idea of sleep. I say, 'Your lids are closing, you can not open them again. Your arms feel heavy, so do your legs. You can not feel anything. Your hands are motionless. You see nothing, you are going to sleep.' And I add in a commanding tone, 'Sleep.' This word often turns the balance. The eyes close and the patient sleeps or is at least influenced."[4]

---

*It should be noted, however, that Liebeault and Bernheim were antedated in recognizing the role of suggestion by such men as Braid, Bertrand, and Faria. The very first allusion to the suggestion factor was probably made by the scientific committee which investigated Mesmer's claims in 1784.

A variation of the subjective method of induction was recently developed by Kline, Watkins, and Moss. According to this method, the subject visualizes various scenes and concentrates on them. These images can be viewed as replacing the usual fixation object. This technique, which is nearly always combined with suggestion, is said to be very valuable in certain instances.

Psychophysical or Mixed Methods

Psychophysical procedures are a combination of physical (or physiological) and psychic methods, and are widely used today. Modern practitioners of hypnosis try to use a combination of methods of hypnotic induction so that they reinforce each other. Trance induction is not a standardized process that can be administered in the same way to everyone. Human personalities have been compared to snowflakes, all seemingly alike and yet infinitely varying, no two exactly the same. What has a profound effect on one subject may have little or none on another. There is no method or technique that always works with everyone or even with the same person on different occasions. By using a mixture of methods the probability of influencing the subject will be increased.

The suggestion method is of prime importance. For whatever psychic or physical technique is used in hypnotic induction it cannot work effectively without suggestion. In this way suggestion can be compared to the fuel for an engine. Suggestion involves some focusing of attention, certainly auditory stimulation and often contains an element of monotony. Contemporary methods of hypnosis combine sight, smell, and hearing fixations with sleep suggestions

applied either sequentially, or more commonly, simultaneously.[5]

An example of the psychophysical method is using any
kind of regular sound, such as the ticking of a watch, a metronome, a clock, or the constant falling of drops of water.
A small microphone can be used to amplify the subject's
own rhythmic heartbeat as a monotonous fixation or conditioned stimulus for sleep. This method can be synchronized
with the appropriate patter. Another variation is to use
intermittent visual stimuli, such as a rotating mirror or a
flashlight, which goes on and off in synchrony with the
metronome. Imagining a peaceful scene or counting backward or forward is also helpful with a combination of either
of these techniques.

The passing over of hands and strokes over the face and
body of the subject usually facilitates hypno-relaxation.

All of these methods can be combined with appropriate
suggestions for relaxation. There are still many more psychophysical techniques, and also many variations of the foregoing
methods. But the successful application of any of them depends upon the psychological characteristics of the subject,
his expectancy, and hypnotist/patient rapport. As has already
been mentioned in a previous section, a specific induction
technique combined with an appropriate suggestion may
bring about a deep hypnosis for one subject in a short time,
but it may fail completely with another subject.

Standing Method

Hypnotizing the subject in the standing position is used
by Cheek and LeCron and they maintain that it is one of
the most valuable methods of inducing hypnosis. The reason

being that the hypnotist can get feedback to help him speed-up the process. It also allows the subject to feel the induction process step by step, and therefore makes him more suggestible.

The standing subject is told to relax his body as much as possible, letting his arms dangle by his sides while looking into the eyes of the hypnotist. At this point he is instructed to either close his eyes or leave them open (whichever is preferred), as he counts backward (aloud) from 100. While he counts the hypnotist places his hands on the shoulders of the subject rocking him around gently in a clockwise circle as he talks to him.

If the subject resists this movement, it means that he is unconsciously resisting the induction. If the subject is easily moved, quick hypnosis may follow. In the former case, a longer talk is required.

As the subject goes on with counting, his voice will usually dwindle off in tone, he may skip over a number or a series of numbers, and finally will have difficulty continuing the count. If the subject's eyes have been open thus far, he is then told to close them. Then the subject may be guided to a seat, or he can continue standing. In either case, the deepening procedure is then begun by the hypnotist.

This method of induction is rather quick, and a very good subject may be hypnotized by the time he has counted only four or five numbers. The average subject may be hypnotized by the time he has reached about "60" in his count.[6]

REFERENCES

1. Gindes, B., *New Concepts of Hypnosis*, p. 128.
2. *Ibid.*, p. 123.
3. *Ibid.*, p. 150.
4. Hippolyte Bernheim, *Suggestive Therapeutics*, trans. C. A. Herter (New York: G. D. Putnam & Sons, 1899), p. 1.
5. Weitzenhoffer, A. "The Induction of Hypnosis," in *Hypnodynamic Psychology*, ed. Milton Kline (New York: Julian Press, Inc., 1955), p. 341.
6. Cheek & LeCron, *Clinical Hypnotherapy*, pp. 30-32.

CHAPTER THIRTEEN

ADVANCED METHODS OF TRANCE INDUCTION

In the previous discussion, "Actual Induction," some basic techniques of induction were explained. In this section, some new methods developed by contemporary researchers of hypnosis are described.

Visual Imagery Technique

This technique, begun by Kline,[1] has been found to be particularly effective with difficult subjects.* It consists of five steps: (1) Each subject is asked to visualize in his mind's eye certain familiar objects. In order, these objects were: (a) a house, (b) a tree, (c) a person, and (d) an animal. For subjects who may have difficulty with visual imagery, other methods have to be applied. These methods should be based upon the principles explained here. (2) Upon completion of the first step, each subject is asked to close his eyes and

---

*This technique was applied to 15 refractory students with satisfactory results. All of these students were resistant to the usual techniques which were applied to them.

picture himself with his eyes open in a chair or lying on a couch. (3) Each subject is then asked to focus on the "image," and the experimenter's comments are directed towards the subject's image (not toward the subject). (4) A simple eye fixation technique is described and related to the eye-closure of the image. Close observation showed that this procedure had an associative effect upon the subject directly. The subject can be asked to confirm eye closure with the image. Even the image can be challenged with the application of the eye catalepsy test. Then after eye closure with the image, deepening techniques are pursued. (5) Direct induction relation with the subject is established and he is told: 'Now you are feeling just like the image, sinking deeper and deeper into sleep, and the image is disapperaring.'

At this point, the subject will go into a light to medium trance. Deepening procedure should then follow.

An interesting variation of picture visualization is explained by Powers[2] as well as Arons.[3] The subject is told to close his eyes and visualize a large blackboard in front of his eyes. He is then asked to envision himself drawing a large circle in the center of the blackboard. Next he is asked to envision drawing a large "X" in the center of the circle. He is then told to "erase" the "X" and delete it from his mind. Again the subject is asked to visualize the empty circle and draw a capital "A" inside it, "erase" it and draw a "B", erase it again, and draw a "C", etc. The hypnotist prompts the subject for the first few letters, then instructs him to continue the visualization of drawing and erasing each letter of the alphabet in turn. The subject is told that when he reaches the end of the alphabet he will be deeply hypnotized. As the subject continues with this visualization, suggestions of deep hypnotic sleep are given simultaneously by the hypnotist.

Powers has found this method particularly effective among individuals with poor concentration. Weitzenhoffer has stated that the visualization method can probably be made extremely effective by choosing scenes or experiences which have deep psychological significance for the subject. Moreover, not only visual imagery, but the other senses may also be used for obtaining effective results. This technique, he adds, appears to be an excellent way for dealing with subjects who are blind.

Star Image

This method, explained by Gindes, is based on a subjective or psychic approach: The subject is seated in a chair and is asked to close his eyes. Then the hypnotist says: "I would like you to visualize in your mind's eye, a star. The star is suspended far—very far in the distance. Please try to concentrate effortlessly and easily—all your attention on that star. Now the star is moving forward, moving forward, closer and closer, becoming larger and larger in your radius of vision. Soon the star will be almost upon you. Now in your own imagination you can visualize that star; it is almost upon you. And now, it is going farther and farther away. It is retracing its path, going farther and farther away into the atmosphere. Soon it will be barely perceptible to you; soon it will be entirely out of your range of vision. When you can no longer see that star, you will be in a deep, sound sleep. You are falling deeper and deeper into sleep now. The star is moving farther and farther away. Now you can hardly see it. Now you cannot see the star at all. It has escaped completely. It is not within your vision any longer. You

Figure 10

cannot see the star; it has escaped your vision completely. Breathe very deeply, with each breath you take, you will fall deeper and deeper into sleep."4 (See figure 10)

The subject will readily slip into a satisfactory state of hypnosis using his own imagination helped by the hypnotist's suggestions. The experienced hypnotist can practice various methods in line with the subject's pattern of thought, gradually guiding him to a satisfactory trance.

The Hour-Glass Technique

The subject is asked to sit in a comfortable chair and an hour glass is placed before him. He is asked to focus his attention on the sand in the hour-glass as it falls from the upper part of the hour-glass to the lower part. Then it is suggested to him that as he watches the slow falling of the sand a dense cloud of drowsiness will envelope him, his eyes will get heavier and heavier and he will eventually close his eyes and fall into a deep sleep. After the upper compartment of the hour-glass has been emptied, the hypnotist should turn the glass upside down, and continue this action again and again until the subject closes his eyes and goes into hypnosis. During this process the hypnotist keeps suggesting to the subject that "as he stares at the falling grains of sand his eyes will become progressively tired." The subject eventually goes under a profound hypno-relaxation. (See figure 11) If an hour-glass is unavailable the subject may be directed to close his eyes and imagine the process. He is told that when he comes to the point where the upper part of the hour-glass has been emptied, he must imagine that the hypnotist has turned it upside down. Eventually he will go under a trance. The hour-glass technique can be applied

Figure 11

as an excellent disguised method for those who are nervous about being hypnotised.

Color Contrast Method

The color contrast method belongs to the objective approach of hypnotic induction, and does not require sleep suggestion. This method was developed by Stokvis[5] who believes that it is well suited for negative subjects. The writer has applied this method on a large number of difficult subjects and has obtained excellent results. The procedure is as follows:

A piece of plain grey cardboard 14x23 centimeters is used and on it two strips of paper 8x3.2 cm. are pasted parallel to each other with a space of 5 millimeters between them. One strip, pasted on the right, should be light blue, the one on the left, light yellow. Both should have a dull finish, and the bottom right hand corner is rounded where the subject will hold the cardboard.

The subject, lying on a couch, is given the cardboard to hold at arm's length (provided that he has normal eyesight). The couch should be in such a position that the light falls on the strips. The subject is asked to look at the slit between the two strips without interruption. While he is doing this, the hypnotist says:

'What do you see exactly on that cardboard?' The subject will naturally reply: 'A piece of gray cardboard on which a yellow strip is pasted on the left, and a blue one on the right of it, with a gray slit between.' The subject is told that, as he continues to watch the picture, especially the slit, he will soon observe some additional colors appearing. These chromatic phenomena, as a general rule, will be observed by any normal person, including the so-called 'red-green dichromatics,' and by all 'anomalous trichromatics'; they consist in appearance of the respective complementary colors along the outside edges of the yellow and blue strips. The hypnotist should say:

'When you see colors appear it is a sign that the hypnotic state is setting in. The appearance of the colors is proof of the hypnotic influence; it is a kind of fatigue phenomenon of the eyes.'

'In the same way that you see these color phenomena, you will observe some other signs of the approaching hypnotic state. Do keep looking at the slit and you will soon see that the inner edge of the blue strip, that is to say, the edge bordering on the slit becomes more intensely blue, while the rest of the blue strip will be a much duller shade.' In precisely the same manner you will notice that the part of the yellow immediately bordering on the gray slit becomes more intensely yellow, while the rest of the yellow strip becomes more faintly yellow. Just keep looking closely. . . . . keep looking fixedly at the slit. . . . . look very closely; you will see something else happen as well. You will also see colors appear in the slit; you will see a yellow border appear along the edge of the blue strip, and a blue border along the edge of the yellow strip. These two newly made colors will touch at about the center of the slit,; now and then they will overlap;

they may even dissapear for a moment or two; because your consciousness is now beginning to waver, owing to the hypnotic condition, which is on the point of setting in.'

Although the subject may feel somewhat skeptical af first, says Stokvis, there is no doubt that by this time he will have abandoned this attitude. For he now sees with his own eyes, step by step, that what is being told to him is also actually happening. The result being that his confidence in the physician will correspondingly increase.

'You remember what I told you just now,' continues the hypnotist, 'that, as you observed the color phenomena, you will find that your eyelids are getting heavier and heavier. . . . . still heavier all the time. . . . . You will feel that you are getting more and more tired. . . . . tired and weary. . . . .and you will soon get so tired that you would just love to shut your eyes. When you feel like that, don't resist. . . . . You may close your eyes.

As has been noted, Stokvis, throughout the induction never mentions the word "sleep." Although this method does not usually produce a very deep hypnosis, the hypnotist can deepen the trance by appropriate methods after the induction. It should be noted, however, that the application of this method is not as simple as it sounds and needs considerable skill.

Instantaneous Technique

Instantaneous or rapid methods of hypnosis are usually used by stage hypnotists. One such method involves giving post-hypnotic suggestion to a person so that on a given signal he will immediately sink into the hypnotic state. If the post-hypnotic signal produces a light trance, the hypnotist applies deepening suggestions and techniques as is usually done following any kind of trance induction.

This method is a variation of one used by some stage hypnotists for hypnotizing their subjects by intimidation and by shouting commands at them to sleep.

Some hypnotists try to apply instantaneous methods of trance induction by suggesting to the subject that they are going to apply pressure to certain "hypnotic nerve centers." Charcot contended that pressure on certain zones of the body helped to induce hypnosis. He listed these hypnotic zones as the root of the nose, the crown of the head, the elbow, and the thumb.[6] According to him if these zones are properly stimulated, hypnosis is produced. Mesmer and various physiologists, including Purkinsje (1787-1869) and Laborde (1831-1903), enumerate principal hypnotic zones as the forehead, the top of the head, the root of the thumbs, the areas adjacent to articulation, the hypochondria, and the ovaries.[7]

There are, of course, no such centers in the body but stage hypnotists, or those who apply this technique, use these so-called "hypnotic" parts for their calming effects on subjects.

There is an instantaneous technique, called "carotid artery pressure method."* This method is dangerous and if used on a person with a sensitive Hering reflex,** may cause carotid arrest or death.*** This method involves putting pressure on the carotid arteries, the receptors start signaling a

---

*The early Greeks believed that the carotid arteries caused drowsiness. Probably this traditional belief has caused the carotid arteries to enter the armamentarium of the hypnotists.
**The neural mechanism that controls respiration automatically by impulses transmitted via the pulmanary fibers of the vagus nerves.
***An article published in *Lancet* on April 2, 1949, on "Deaths from Vagal Inhibitions," by Dr. Keith Simpton, has explained cases in which death has resulted from pressures on the neck.

rise in blood pressure to the brain and the heart is commanded to slow down. As a result the subject's blood supply to his brain is interrupted and he begins to faint. On rare occasions the shock of this may bring about a state of trance but more commonly the stage hypnotist, using this method, will represent to his audience the faint or collapse resulting from the application of this procedure as an instantaneous trance.[8]

It has also been shown that if the blood vessels in the neck are pressured, the brain will be deprived of oxygen and therefore, a state of dull awareness, which is actually a hypnoidal state, will be produced.

The stage hypnotist will give the subject proper suggestions while he is passing from the state of consciousness into unconsciousness.

This method has no place in ethical hypnosis and its application should be completely rejected even by physician-hypnotists.

Disguised Method

Erickson and Kubie[9] have developed a very interesting technique to induce hypnosis on a subject who is not willing to be hypnotized. The first step in the process was to contact the roomate of the unwilling patient and gain her approval to cooperate with them in the hypnotic procedure. Then the patient was asked, as a special favor, to act as a chaperone while her roommate, a patient of Erickson, was supposedly hypnotized. During the hypnosis session Erickson directed the patient (chaperone), to pay close attention to the process, because she herself might at some future time want to try it too. According to the authors, the hypnotic procedure was carried out as follows:

Upon entering the office, the two girls were seated in adjacent chairs and a prolonged, tedious, and laborious series of suggestions was given to the roommate who soon developed an excellent trance, thereby setting an effective example for the intended patient. During the course of the trance, suggestions were given to the roommate in such a way that by imperceptible degrees they were accepted by the patient as applying to her. The two girls were seated not far apart, in identical chairs, and such a manner that they adopted more or less similar postures as they faced the hypnotist; also they were so placed that the hypnotist could unobtrusively observe either or both of them continuously. In this way it was possible to give a suggestion which coincided with the patient's respiratory movements. With careful, repeated, suggestions it was possible finally to see that any suggestion given to the roommate with regard to her respiration was automatically performed by the patient as well. Similarly, the patient having been observed placing her hand on her thigh, the suggestion was given to the roommate that she place her hand upon her thigh too and that she should feel it resting there. Such maneuvers gradually and cumulatively brought the patient into a close identification with her roommate, so that gradually anything said to the roommate applied to the patient as well.

Interspersed with this were other maneuvers. For instance, the hypnotist would turn to the patient and say casually, 'I hope you are not getting too tired waiting.' In subsequent suggestions to the roommate that she was tired, the patient herself would thereupon feel increasing fatigue without any realization that this was because of a suggestion which had been given to her. Gradually, it then became possible for the hypnotist to make suggestions to the roommate, while looking directly at the patient, thus creating in the patient an impulse to respond, just as anyone feels when someone looks at one, while addressing a question or comment to another person.

Technical suggestions were given to the patient to the effect that she should allow herself to be hypnotized again, that she should go into a sound and deep trance, and that if she had any resistance toward such a trance she should make the hypnotist aware of it after the trance had developed, whereupon she could then decide whether or not to continue in the trance. The purpose of these suggestions was merely to make certain that the patient would again allow herself to be hypnotized with full confidence that she could, if she chose, disrupt the trance at any time. This illusion of self-determination made it certain that the hypnotist would be able to swing the patient into a trance. Once in that condition, he was confident that he could keep her there until his therapeutic aims had been achieved.

It took the authors an hour and a half to develop a deep trance in the patient. As was explained, the subject was not addressed directly, and suggestions of sleep, relaxation, fatigue, etc. were administered.

If there is an audience present where a hypnotic induction is taking place, a number of people may be induced with the application of this method. Furthermore, a sudden shift of attention to some members of the audience with a strong command of "Sleep!" may put them under hypnosis.

REFERENCES

1.   Kline, M. V., "A Visual Imagery Technique for the Induction of Hypnosis in Certain Refractory Subjects," *Journal of Psychology*, 35: 227-28, 1953.
2.   Powers, M., *Advanced Techniques of Hypnosis* (No. Hollywood,CA: Wilshire Book Co., 1953), p. 48.
3.   Arons, *New Master Course in Hypnotism*, pp. 134-36.
4.   Gindes, *New Concepts of Hypnosis*, p. 162.
5.   Stokvis, B., "A Simple Hypnotizing Technique with the Aid of Color-Contrast Action," *Amer. Journal of Psychiatry*, LIII, No.2 (June , 1959), 380-81.
6.   Gindes, *New Concepts of Hypnosis*, p. 128.
7.   Dauven, J., *The Powers of Hypnosis* (New York: Scarborough Book Re-issue, 1980), p.223.

8. Udolf, *Handbook of Hypnosis for Professionals,* p. 72.
9. Erickson, M. and L. S. Kubie, "The Successful Treatment of a Case of Acute Hysterical Discussion by a Return under Hypnosis to a Critical Phase of Childhood," *Psychoanalysis Quarterly,* 10: 358-609, 1941.

CHAPTER FOURTEEN

DEEPENING THE TRANCE

Deepening the trance of the subject to his maximum degree of hypnotic susceptibility is more difficult than the induction of hypnosis. "Deep hypnosis" is that level of hypnosis which permits the subject to function adequately and directly at an unconscious level of awareness without interference by the conscious mind.[1]

Deepening suggestions are simply a continuation of the induction procedure and are commonly followed until the subject appears to be as deep as his hypnotic capacity permits. A very good subject may enter a deep trance in the course of a very short time, possibly in only three or four minutes; such a subject is among those 20 per cent who are susceptible to deep hypnosis. With others, a longer time should be spent to deepen their trance.

Arons states that he has found in his experience that practical considerations require a subject be projected into a workable degree of hypnosis in six to ten sessions. He adds that the average subject can reach the maximum possible degree of his hypnotic capacity within that time.[2]

Erickson has found that "subjects who have experienced hypnosis frequently over a long period of time, and who have also produced a great variety of hypnotic phenomena, are by far the better subjects."[3]

Generally speaking, the deepening procedure should include suggesting to the subject that his relaxation is becoming progressively deeper and deeper. Silence for about 10 to 15 minutes is very effective for spontaneously deepening the trance of the subject. Before starting the period of silence, the hypnotist simply tells the subject that he is going to leave him for a few minutes so he may go deeper into the trance state and become more and more relaxed.

Another method of deepening the trance is when the hypnotist tells the subject that he is going to touch him on the shoulder with both hands and push him deeper into hypnosis. This statement should be accompanied by suggestions that the subject will go deeper and deeper into the trance state and the hypnotist may at the same time count from 1 to 3 or from 1 to 5. Stroking the forehead of the subject in a gentle, soothing manner accompanied by the suggestion of going deeper into hypnosis is found to be very effective—especially with children.

It should be noted that whenever the hypnotist is going to touch the subject for any purpose, he must warn him earlier in order to avoid startling him.

Making the subject follow a variety of ideomotor and ideosensory activities also greatly helps the depth of hypnosis. For instance, when one suggests to the subject that if he thinks, feels, and imagines with each breath that he is going deeper and deeper into relaxation, he will really drift more and more into relaxation. By the same token, visual imagery suggestions are also very helpful in deepening the trance of the subject. For example, the subject is asked to visualize that he has entered his bed, is very exhausted, and is sinking into an extremely deep sleep.

In addition to the above mentioned general techniques for deepening the trance, there are other techniques which may achieve the same result. Some examples follow:

The Escalator Technique

Subjective or cognitive suggestions are very valuable in deepening the trance. One such method is having the subject imagine that he is at the top of a long escalator, holding its railings. Then the suggestion should be given that with every step he is carried down the escalator, he becomes more and more relaxed and that the further the escalator moves down, the deeper and deeper he sinks into hypnosis. The descent of the escalator is symbolic of his descent into deeper levels of trance.

It is important to take the psychological characteristics of a subject into account in making psychic or cognitive suggestions. For example, if a subject has a height phobia (acrophobia), then an ascending escalator might be suggested instead. In this case the phrase "going farther into hypnosis" would be used in lieu of "deeper."

Another variation of this method is to tell the subject to visualize that he is in an elevator on a high floor such as the 15th floor of a high rise building. Then it is suggested that the elevator is going to move down, and as it goes down, deeper and deeper, he is relaxed. As each number on the landing gets smaller and smaller, he will go deeper and deeper into relaxation. When finally the elevator stops at the lowest floor, he will be in the deepest possible state of relaxation.

Vogt's Fractionation Method

The fractionation method developed by Vogt[4] is one of the most effective methods for deepening the state of trance. It is very practical and valuable when other methods have failed. It is applied in two ways: (1) hypnotization and de-hypnotization. (2) Feedback of the subject's most relaxing sensations.

In essence, the subject is hypnotized and de-hypnotized several times within the same session with the suggestion that on each subsequent hypnosis he will go "even deeper into relaxation than before." The subsequent hypnosis may be induced by a post-hypnotic cue or by a separate induction procedure as feedback using the subject's thoughts, feelings, and sensations he experienced at the moment of his maximal relaxation. The reasoning behind this procedure is that each hypnotization makes the subject a little more suggestible and brings about a deeper hypnosis at the next attempt. This feedback technique is often very effective, since it permits the hypnotist to avoid suggesting experiences which the subject may not have enjoyed, and also those experiences to which he may be consciously or unconsciously resistant.

It is a good idea to tell the subject a few seconds before waking him that in a moment he will be told to awaken. But he will immediately feel very drowsy again, so that he will find it very difficult to keep his eyes open. After trying to arouse himself, he will feel sleepy again and sink into a much deeper sleep than before.

Hypnotization and de-hypnotization of the subject and the process of "feedback" may be repeated on the average of six times and as many as ten times. Every now and then the subject may be given a "silence period" for about 10 to 15 minutes. Whenever the operator is going to leave the subject for a "silence period," he has to give him a post-hypnotic suggestion in the following manner:

"I am going to leave you for a few minutes. While I leave you, nothing can interrupt your trance. You will remain in a deep, deep, relaxed state as each minute passes by. And with every breath that you take, you will find yourself becoming more deeply relaxed. Upon my return, you will be in a deep, deep state of relaxation."

When the hypnotist returns to the subject, he has to resume talking to him very slowly (whisperlike), and then gradually elevate the level of his voice to a lullaby tone— otherwise the subject will be startled.

The fractionation technique can be used in conjunction with the hand levitation method for subsequent inductions even when the hand levitation is applied in the deepening phase of the previous trance state.

The Confusion Method

The confusion method, a very effective technique for deepening the trance, was developed by Erickson. This method is based on the giving of suggestions and instructions which confuse the subject. The subject is continuously given a host of contradictory suggestions and is compelled to shift from one task or idea to another. The rationale behind this technique is that when the subject encounters the contradictory suggestions of the hypnotist and develops uncertainty about what is expected of him, to escape such confusion, he sinks into the lethargy of a deep hypnosis.

The hypnotist makes contradictory but meaningful statements, but the subject feels that he has not enough time to establish the logical character of the suggestions. As an example, Erickson explains the application of the confusion method to hand levitation. It is suggested to the subject that his right hand is rising and his left hand is immobile. Then immediately, it is said that the left hand is rising, and the right hand is immobile. After this contradictory suggestion, the hypnotist states that one of the subject's hands is rising, while the other is pressing down; one is feeling warm, and the other is feeling cold. Then the one which had the warm feeling is said to have cold feeling, and vice-versa. The hypnotist then returns to the initial suggestion. The important point in the confusion technique is that the contradictory suggestions should be stated rapidly, with insistence, and confidence.

Erickson believes that this technique is very effective with highly intelligent individuals and those who are unconsciously willing to be hypnotized but consciously unwilling.[5]

A variation of this technique is suggested by Weitzenhoffer: The subject is told to count backwards slowly from 100 and to pay a subliminal attention to what the hypnotist says while he counts. After the subject has begun counting the hypnotist gives him suggestions for relaxation which result in heaviness of the eyes and finally eye closure. LeCron believes that before the subject reaches zero, he will sink into a deep hypnosis. While the subject continues counting, hand levitation is suggested. Naturally, at this time, the subject becomes confused and wonders what is expected of him. The hypnotist should be very quick in recognizing this point, and tells the subject that when he reaches ten more numbers, he will lose track of his count.[6]

The confusion technique is said to be not only helpful in inducing the trance state, but particularly helpful for age regression.*

The Rehearsal Method

The rehearsal or repetition technique was started by Erickson[7] and was elaborated by Arons.[8] The subject is simply told to pretend that he is going into hypnosis, and to act in a cooperative way to the hypnotist's suggestions. In other words, the subject is asked to believe that he is an actor in a play, and is playing the role of a hypnotized subject.

Then the subject is given the eye catalepsy, arm catalepsy and other similar tests, particularly those dealing with muscular inability. Little by little, a kind of doubt is developed in the subject about whether he actually is in hypnosis or not, and whether he can open his eyes, or lower his arm or not. It is natural that when a person assumes inability to do something, he is doubtful whether he can really do it, unless he makes an effort. After waking, if the subject's feelings and sensations are indicative of the state of hypnosis, like numbness or tingling in the fingers, time distortion, and feelings of heaviness, lightness, or floating, these may be good reason to believe that he has been really hypnotized. Then the hypnotist may give him some tests of the eye and arm catalepsy in successive sessions.

As Arons has put it, the idea behind this method is similar to the idea of a person lying constantly about the same thing. After a while, he is not sure whether he is telling the truth or not. Therefore, whether the subject actually

---

*See Chapter 21.

carries out a certain act or only pretends to carry it out, it causes similar patterns to develop in the brain, and the act becomes a reality.

Post-Hypnotic Technique

This technique also initiated by Erickson[9] for deepening the trance is very similar and practical. Before waking the subject, the operator will tell him that during the next session, he will go into a deeper trance much more quickly and easily. Although not all subjects respond to this method, it often proves of immense value.

Initially, a simple post-hypnotic suggestion is given to the subject who is in a light trance and when the subject goes into the second trance in compliance with the post-hypnotic suggestion of the first trance, suggestions may be given to deepen it. The procedure is repeated and a third trance, still deeper, can result—until sufficient repetitions bring a deep hypnosis.

This method is very common and most hypnotists will give such a suggestion to their subjects as a routine, whether deepening of the trance is needed or not.

REFERENCES

1. Erickson, "Deep Hypnosis and its Induction," in *Experimental Hypnosis,* ed. Leslie M. Lecron (New York: The Macmillan Co., 1954), p.80.
2. Arons, *New Master Course in Hypnotism,* p. 152.
3. Weitzenhoffer, *General Techniques of Hypnotism,* p. 271.
4. *Zur Kenntni's des Wesens und der Psychologischen Bedeutung des Hypnotismus,* quoted in William S. Kroger, Clinical and Experimental Hypnosis, p. 82.
5. Erickson in LeCron, *Experimental Hypnosis,* pp. 98-102.
6. *Experimental Hypnosis,* quoted in Weitzenhoffer, *General Tech-*

niques of Hypnotism, p. 275.
7. Erickson in LeCron, *Experimental Hypnosis,* pp. 102-8.
8. Arons, *New Master Course in Hypnotism,* pp. 132-34.
9. Erickson in LeCron, *Experimental Hypnosis,* pp. 108-9.

CHAPTER FIFTEEN

MEASUREMENT OF THE DEPTH OF HYPNOSIS

As it has already been mentioned, there is no similarity between hypnosis and natural sleep, but the depth of these two states are analogous. Hypnosis, like natural sleep, occurs in degrees. A great deal of investigation has been done on measuring of the depth of hypnosis and a variety of scales have been proposed for this purpose. The most well-known and practical of these scales seem to be the Davis-Husband scale, Lecron-Bordeaux scale, and Arons scale. What these authors have done is to arrange hypnotic phenomena in descending order of simplicity and have assigned numbers to them. Despite the fact that these scales are criticized by some, they are now gaining popularity and acceptance. The Davis-Husband scale divides hypnosis into five major levels of trance depth: insusceptible, hypnoidal, light trance, medium trance, and somnambulism or deep trance. Each of these five levels is further subdivided into 22 relevant hypnotic phenomena in descending order of simplicity, to which numerical values from 0 to 30 are assigned. To determine the level of hypnosis (with the exception of the insusceptible and the hypnoidal divisions) the operator will give the subject the suggestions in listed order. When resistance is met and no further phenomena is produced, the previous phenomenon in the listed order will show the hypnotic depth of the subject. For example, if the subject responds to "glove anesthesia" but does not show "partial amnesia," he is assigned a depth level of 11 and his trance is considered "light."

Davis-Husband Scale[1]

DEPTH	SCORE	TEST SUGGESTION AND RESPONSES
Insusceptible	0	
Hypnoidal	1	
	2	Relaxation
	3	Fluttering of the eyelids
	4	Closing of the eyes
	5	Complete physical relaxation
Light Trance	6	Catalepsy of the eyes
	7	Limb catalepsies
	10	Rigid catalepsies
	11	Glove anesthesia
Medium Trance	13	Partial amnesia
	15	Posthypnotic anesthesia
	17	Personality changes
	18	Simple posthypnotic suggestions
	20	Kinesthetic delusions; complete amnesia
Deep Trance	21	Ability to open the eyes without affecting the trance
(Somnambulism)	23	Bizarre posthypnotic suggestions
	25	Complete somnambulism
	26	Positive visual hallucinations, posthypnotic
	27	Positive auditory hallucinations. posthypnotic
	28	Systemized posthypnotic amnesias
	29	Negative auditory hallucinations
	30	Negative visual hallucinations, hyperesthesia

LeCron and Bordeaux modified the Davis-Husband scale by adding a sixth category of depth called a plenary trance, and increasing the numbers assigned to each subdivision in the list to 50 as against 23 in the Davis-Husband scale. Two points are assigned to each hypnotic phenomenon, the total of which reaches 100. The plenary trance, according to the LeCron-Bordeaux scale, is a hypnotic level even deeper than a somnambulistic state, in which animation and all spontaneous activity eliminated.

The main difference between the Davis-Husband and LeCron-Bordeaux scales is that in the latter a subject in one degree of hypnosis may comply with suggestions to other degrees and yet fail to show some of the symptoms of his own level of trance depth. In the Davis-Husband scale a subject cannot show a given symptom unless he has complied with all the suggestions preceding it in the listed order. Conversely, a subject cannot comply with suggestions below the one he failed to show. Another difference between the Davis-Husband and LeCron-Bordeaux scales is that the former scale regards analgesia(glove anesthesia) as a characteristic of a medium trance, while the latter considers it as a symptom of a light trance.

LeCron-Bordeaux Scale[2]

DEPTH OF HYPNOSIS	WEIGHT	CRITERION SYMPTOM
Insusceptible	0	Subject fails to react in any way
Hypnoidal	1	Physical relaxation
	2	Drowsiness apparent
	3	Fluttering of the eyelids
	4	Closing of the eyes
	5	Mental relaxation, partial lethargy of the mind
	6	Heaviness of limbs
Light trance	7	Catalepsy of the eyes
	8	Partial limb catalepsy
	9	Inhibition of small muscle groups
	10	Slower and deeper breathing, slower pulse
	11	Strong lassitude (disinclin-

		ation to move, speak, think, or act)
	12	Twitching of mouth or jaw during induction
	13	Rapport between subject and operator
	14	Simple post-hypnotic suggestions heeded
	15	Involuntary start or eye twitch on waking
	16	Personality changes
	17	Feeling of heaviness throughout entire body
	18	Partial feeling of detachment
Medium trance	19	Recognition of trance (difficult to describe but definately felt)
	20	Complete muscular inhibitions (kinaesthetic delusions)
	21	Partial amnesia
	22	Glove anesthesia
	23	Tactile illusions
	24	Gustatory illusions
	25	Olfactory illusions
	26	Hyperacuity to atmospheric conditions
	27	Complete catalepsy of limbs or body
Deep or somnambulistic trance	28	Ability to open eyes without affecting trance
	29	Fixed stare when eyes are open; pupilary dilation
	30	Somnambulism
	31	Complete amnesia
	32	Systemized post-hypnotic amnesia
	33	Complete anesthesia
	34	Post-hypnotic anesthesia
	35	Bizarre post-hypnotic suggestions needed
	36	Uncontrolled movements of eyeballs—eye coordination lost
	37	Sensation of lightness, floating, swinging, of being bloated or swollen, detached feeling

	38	Rigidity and lag in muscular movements and reactions
	39	Fading and increase in cycles of the sound of operator's voice (like radio station fading in and out)
	40	Control of organic body functions (heart beat, blood pressure, digestion, etc.)
	41	Recall of lost memories (hypermnesia)
	42	Age regression
	43	Positive visual hallucinations; posthypnotic
	44	Negative visual hallucinations; post-hypnotic
	45	Positive auditory hallucinations; post-hypnotic
	46	Negative auditory hallucinations; post-hypnotic
	47	Stimulation of dreams (in trance or post-hypnotic in natural sleep)
	48	Hyperaesthesia
	49	Color sensations experienced
Plenary trance	50	Stuporous condition in which all spontaneous activity is inhibited. Somnambulism can be developed by suggestion to that effect

Arons[3] has divided the hypnotic depth into six stages. These stages are as follows:

1) Hypnoidal or lethargic stage
2) Light sleep
3) Sleep
4) Deep sleep
5) Somnambulism
6) Profound Somnambulism

According to Arons the first three are called mnesic (memory-retaining) stages and the last three are termed amnesic (no memory) stages.

Arons states that in the first two levels the subject may not be able to open his eyes, to bend or lower his arm (partial catalepsy) upon challenge. In the third stage, the subject will not be able to rise, sit down, or to speak if he is told to and he can not articulate specific words or sounds upon challenge. But he will not forget them in this stage of trance depth (third stage). In the first two stages of trance depth only negligible post-hypnotic reactions are possible.

In the third stage it is possible to produce glove anesthesia (insensitivity to pain), partial amnesia, incomplete hallucinations, and simple post-hypnotic suggestions.

In the fourth stage, a subject will forget a number, his name, and almost anything suggested to him. Other symptoms of this stage are analgesia, opening the eyes without the danger of awakening, smell and taste hallucinations, execution of post-hypnotic suggestions, re-induction of the hypnotic state by command or signal, and amnesia for several hours after the trance termination.

In the fifth stage, the subject enters the somnambulistic state of trance. The symptoms of this stage are complete anesthesia, complete or selective amnesia, both in the hypnotic and post-hypnotic states, positive and sometimes negative hallucinations.

The sixth stage of trance depth is characterized by profound somnambulism in which all the hypnotic phenomena including negative hallucinations are possible.

Some authors, such as Klint[4] and de Milechnin[5] among others have come to the conclusion that trance stages are not exact. They have found that too often the stages of the trance overlap. The authors conclude that the scales in use do not sufficiently take into account, the psychodynamics of the hypnotic situation and the personality traits of the subject. Some subjects, for example, can have hallucinations with greater ease in a certain stage of trance while some can produce hallucinations in earlier stages of trance depth than expected, while still others are not able to manifest hallucinations to the degree expected.

At any rate, these critical comments are insufficient to diminish the value of the scales explained above. Weitzenhoffer[6] believes that among the above-mentioned scales, the Davis-Husband scale is the most practical.

If we agree with the aforementioned authors, that the psychodynamics of the hypnotic environment and the personality structure of the subject are not easy to evaluate, then we should also accept that the development of a crystal-clear scale to measure the exact degree of depth of hypnosis is not feasible. Therefore, the scales in use are probably the most reliable tools in gauging the depth of hypnosis. Naturally, a combination of the application of suggestibility tests and the experience of the hypnotist, will make the utilization of the scales more practical and exact.

REFERENCES

1. Erickson, "Deep Hypnosis and its Induction," *Experimental Hypnosis,* LeCron, ed. (New York: The Macmillan Company, 1954), p.80.
2. LeCron and Bordeaux, *Hypnotism Today,* pp.64-67.
3. Arons, *New Master Course in Hypnosis,* pp.101-3.
4. Kline, "Hypnotic Retrogression: A Neurophysiological Theory of Age Regression and Progression," *Journal of Clinical and Experimental Hypnosis,* 1: 21-28, 1953.
5. de Milechnin, "Concerning the Concepts of Hypnotic Depth," *Journal of Clinical and Experiemental Hypnosis,* 3:243-52, 1955.
6. Weitzenhoffer, *Hypnotism: An Objective Study in Susceptibility* (New York:John Wiley and Sons, Inc., 1953), p.59.

CHAPTER SIXTEEN

HYPNOTIC DEPTH TESTS

When a subject is hypnotized and his hypnotic trance has been deepened, the hypnotist may wish to measure the depth of his trance. To do this, the operator should apply some tests to the subject using the symptoms mentioned in the scales explained in the previous chapter. These tests are as follows:

Eye Catalepsy Test

In hypnosis "catalepsy" is the term used for any muscular condition in which the subject is unable to voluntarily move a certain member of his body.

An eye catalepsy test may be applied to measure the hypnotizability of the subject as well as gauging the depth of his hypnotic trance when hypnotized.

When the subject is hypnotized, the hypnotist should address him and state: "Your eyes are closed and you are so relaxed that the muscles around your eyes are flaccid, and limp. Your eyelids have become so heavy that they feel as if they are made of lead. Your eyelids feel glued together so that even though you try hard to open them, you will not be able to do so. You feel that you are losing control of the muscles which open and close your eyes. Your eyelids are tightly shut, and you can not open them but don't try. Don't try until I count to three. On the count of three you will try to open your eyes but you will not be able to do so. Now, one, your eyes are sticking fast. Two, they are glued tightly together. Three, the lids are locked tightly together. They are shut tight, tight, very tight. You can not open your eyes. The harder you try to open them, the tighter the lids stick together. Try. But you can not. Now relax, relax, and go deeper and deeper into relaxation."

The hypnotist should not allow more than two or three seconds for the subject to try. The inability of the subject to open his eyes indicates that he has already passed the early stages of the light state of hypnotic trance. The deepening of the trance and following that the next test should then be given.

Another variation of the eye catalepsy test is used to evaluate the hypnotizability of the subject. For this purpose the subject is told: "I would like you to close your eyes and relax your body and just listen to my voice effortlessly. As you do so, your eyelids become heavy, very heavy. Soon you will find it difficult to open your eyes because they are becoming heavy, heavy, and heavier. Your eyelids are getting so heavy that you feel they are glued together. They are so tightly closed that you will find it very difficult to open your eyes when I tell you to try. Now your eyes are becoming more tightly closed. They are locked together. They simply lock tighter and tighter and tighter. Your eyes are shut tight. They are stuck fast. You will try to open them but you are so relaxed and your eyes are so heavy that you cannot do that. The harder you try to open them the tighter they lock. Try to open them, but you cannot. You cannot open your eyes. All right, now relax, completely relax."

After this test has been successfully applied, the hypnotist may count to three and instruct the subject to open his eyes; or he may continue the process of the trance using deepening techniques.

Arm Catalepsy

The hypnotist instructs the subject to stretch one of his arms out, straighten it and form a tight fist. With one hand he holds the subject's fist and squeezes it lightly. Then he grasps the subject's elbow with his other hand and gives it an outward pull. While doing that the hypnotist addresses the subject and says: "Imagine that the muscles of your arm are beginning to get tense and rigid. I lock your arm at the elbow (squeezing it lightly), and it becomes stiff, stiffer even stiffer, just like a bar of iron. Now, you feel the muscles of your arm contract and it stiffens up. Every muscle in your arm is getting rigid, rigid as a bar of steel. Your arm is now so stiff that you can not bend it. The more you try to bend it, the stiffer it gets. You can not move it. Try. You can't. . . "

After the successful completion of this test, the operator continues: "Now, as I stroke your arm (while stroking it gently), the tension will leave your arm, it becomes loose and limp and you will be able to bend it and you may put it in your lap. Then you go into a deeper hypnosis. That is it!"

If the depth of the trance is appropriate for the test and the hypnotist administers it properly, the test will undoubtedly succeed.

A variation of this test is when the hypnotist raises the subject's arm, extends it forward, and instructs him to form a tight fist. The hypnotist then squeezes the wrist, elbow, and shoulder joints of the subject with the intention of making them stiff. While doing so he states the following: "I am going to lock your arm at the wrist, elbow, and shoulder.

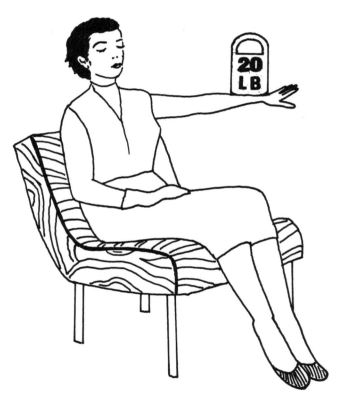

Figure 12

Now, you feel that the muscles inside your arm are tensing up, becoming rigid and stiff. You can feel that all the muscles of your arm are locked together and your arm becomes like a bar of steel. You can neither move your arm nor lower it. I am going to count to three. On the count of three, you will try to lower your arm but will find it impossible. Even if I try to push your arm down, it will bounce back. The harder you try to push your arm down, the more it will bounce back. One—your arm is stiff and rigid, you cannot lower it. Two—it is stiff just like a piece of iron. Three—you cannot lower it. Try—but you cannot. All right now, believing you cannot lower your arm, stop trying. Now, I will stroke your arm (the hypnotist gently strokes the arm), it will become loose and limp and you will be able to lower it. Now put it in your lap and go into a still deeper relaxation."

Amnesia

Amnesia (inability to recall) is one of the characteristics of the human mind, and one of the common experiences of everyday life. Sometimes we forget temporarily the name of an intimate friend who we have known for a long time. Studies have shown that amnesia occurs in hypnosis[1] either spontaneously or it can be suggested to the hypnotized subject. When anaesthesia is produced the subject may not be aware of what has happened during hypnosis, but the recollections are not completely forgotton. Highly susceptible subjects can recall (through re-hypnotization) almost everything that has occurred during the hypnotic session. Some gradually forget all (complete amnesia) or some of their experiences (partial amnesia) during hypnosis. Still others, even when deeply hypnotized, do not produce amnesia because the structure of their character requires them to maintain control. In such cases, a solution proposed by Wolberg[2] is to suggest to the subject that he remembers some minor aspects of the trance, but that he have amnesia for the rest of it.

In the past it was believed that spontaneous amnesia usually occurred only in highly susceptible subjects. This has now been disproved. It has been said that as dreams are generally difficult to recall, so it is with the hypnotic subject who forgets details of the hypnotic session.According to recent studies, spontaneous amnesia is not regarded as an inherent indication of depth or susceptibility but is a specific hypnotic phenomenon. Hilgard and Cooper[3] found in a volunteer/student group that spontaneous amnesia occurred in 7 per cent, and suggested amnesia produced the phenomenon in 35 per cent of the subjects. In this study no relationship was found between traditional signs of increased susceptibility and the occurrence of spontaneous amnesia.

Suggested amnesia, unlike spontaneous amnesia, is positively correlated to susceptibility and depth of hypnosis. A highly susceptible subject who responds well to suggestion will produce suggested amnesia. This, however, need not necessarily be produced by the hypnotist. With suggested amnesia the hypnotist can control the amnesic condition. He can, for example, cause a subject to forget one hypnotic incident and recall another before terminating induction.

Post-hypnotic amnesia seems to be due to a direct or implied suggestion to forget what has occurred during the hypnotic session. By the same token, if the subject is asked to remember what has occurred during hypnosis, he will develop no amnesia (providing he finds the suggestion acceptable). Wolberg[4] believes that even a so-called complete post-hypnotic amnesia is not perfect. Often subjects will remember hypnotic incidents, but will consider them a result of their own fantasies.

In hypnotherapy amnesia serves as a defensive tool to protect the patient from the outpouring of emotions tied to a traumatic event in the past. Suggestions given to the patient during hypnosis will be effective even though amnesia has been produced, because it operates through the unconscious part of the mind.

Kroger gives the following instructions for producing amnesia: "You may find it very convenient to forget everything that I suggested. Imagine that your mind is like a blackboard that has just had everything erased." Another technique is to say: "After you open your eyes, you will have no recollection of what I said to you while you were in a relaxed state. However, all the suggestions I gave you will be effectively carried out as specified."[5]

Anaesthesia

Anaesthesia,* one of the most interesting phenomena of hypnosis can be produced in the deeper stages of the hypnotic trance. Not only amnesia, but almost all of the interesting hypnotic phenomena, such as hallucination, personality change, regression, etc. will be developed during deep hypnosis; and the degree of hypnoanaesthesia usually varies with the depth of hypnosis reached and the extent of

---

*Anaesthesia actually means loss of sensory perception but in hypnosis parlance it is used synonomously with "analgesia," which means absence of sensitivity to pain.

motivation of the subject.[6]

Hypnoanaesthesia, in contrast to chemical anaesthesia, is in no way harmful to the patient. Unlike chemical anaesthesia which can lead to post-operative nausea, drug poisoning, post-operative shock, and patient anxiety; hypnoanaesthesia does not have any such disadvantages. Hypnotic anaesthesia is especially beneficial for those people who, because of prior illnesses or organic defects, cannot be given chemical anaesthesia.

The practical value of hypnoanaesthesia, however, is limited by the number of people (10%) who are susceptible to the degree of hypnotic depth which promotes anaesthesia; and also by the time required to produce the condition (several conditioning sessions for most people—making it expensive).

Anaesthesia can be easily induced in any part of the body of a good subject e.g., a hand, an arm, a limb, or even a certain area of the body. Anaesthesia can be induced in all the senses but is most easily produced on the skin. Hypnotic anaesthesia, or insensitivity to pain, is not produced as a result of elimination of pain in the tissues or by blocking the pathways of pain. Rather, it eliminates the awareness of pain by acting on the cortical processes involved. In other words, hypnoanaesthesia eliminates the perception of pain, not the pain itself.

Functional blindness is another manifestation of hypnotic anaesthesia and may be developed in the eyes. This, of course, does not mean that hypnoanesthesia will influence the physiological mechanism of the eyes; sight will be inhibited because visual images will not reach the brain. Erickson[7] has produced visual anaesthesia in a number of subjects; they saw (hallucinated) the colors red, yellow, green, and blue on white sheets of paper. Erickson[8] also produced fuctional deafness to the extent that subjects did not hear the operator's voice at certain times.

Glove Anaesthesia

Probably the most general method to induce hypno-analgesia is the "glove anaesthesia" technique. Glove anaes-thesia refers to the loss of tactile sensation in the hand from the wrist to the finger tips. After glove anaesthesia is induced, the hand will be numb, wooden-like, and insensitive to burn-ing and pricking just as if the hand was thickly gloved or had been injected with an anaesthetic agent. Although one ob-jective study showed that glove anaesthesia required only a moderate depth of trance, it is often characteristic of deep hypnosis.[9]

Hypnoanaesthesia is not suggested directly. It should be induced by using "imagination power" rather than "will power." For instance, it is incorrect to suggest, "try to feel your hand becoming senseless" or "I want your hand to get numb." Rather, the hypnotist will gently rub the back of the hand and say: "In a short while you will feel that all sensation has gone from your hand. Imagine that your hand is getting numb, cold and insensitive, as when you put it in a bucket of ice cubes. As you envision this, you feel your hand developing a numb, wooden, and heavy feeling—as when it goes to sleep. Right now you feel that your hand has lost all feeling. Very soon you will find that you will not feel any pain in your hand. It is completely numb and insensitive. I am going to count to three. When I reach the number "three" your hand will be completely insensitive to pain. There will be absolutely no sense of pain at all. One . . . your hand is getting more and more numb, and you are losing all feeling, all sense of pain in it. Two . . . your hand is so insensitive that it is impossible for you to feel any sensation in it. There is no feeling of any kind in it. Three . . . your hand has lost all feeling. It is absolutely numb and insensitive. It seems that it has been detached from your body and you have no sense in it whatsoever. You cannot feel any pain in your hand . . . no matter what I do with it. You cannot feel any pain in it. It is completely numb and insensitive."

To test anaesthesia of the hand concurrently with the suggestions of no pain, the operator pierces the subject's hand with a pin or he lifts up the flap of the skin on the back of the hand with a pair of scissors. Or he may pinch the back of the subject's hand. He may also instruct the subject to pinch his anaesthetized hand with the other one.

Another test of hand anaesthesia is to put a burning candle or a flaming match (for obvious reasons this test requires an experienced operator) under the palm and fingers of the subject, moving it back and forth while carefully avoiding any one spot on the hand to prevent tissue damage.

Hand levitation may also be used to develop glove anaesthesia.

Glove anaesthesia can be transferred to any area of the body desired. Sparks has explained an interesting method for transferring anaesthesia from the hand to the area requiring insensitivity in dental procedures. This procedure can be developed, according to Sparks, as follows:

> Once anaesthesia is developed in the hand, the numbness can be made to leave the hand by appropriate suggestions as the hand is rubbed against the cheek or jaw. When the jaw is completely numb on the basis of pre-arrangement with the dentist the hand can be lowered as a signal for the dental procedure to start.

During the dental work the patient can watch a movie or experience any other pleasant activity through imagination. The numbness will stay in the jaw all during the proceedings, and there will be no pain or other after-effects. If it is suggested, there is little or no bleeding from surgery and healing takes place much sooner. The dental surgery under hypnoanaesthesia becomes a pleasant experience for the person who develops this ability.[10]

Talking in Hypnosis Without Awakening

Hypnotized subjects can talk—even carry on a complex conversation without coming out of the trance. Nevertheless, some subjects may wake up, or the depth of their trance may be lightened, if made to talk. To counteract this effect, the subject may first be asked some simple questions that he can answer by nodding his head—questions dealing with the weather, the day of the week, etc. Then he is gradually asked objective questions such as his name, his job, etc. before the operator reaches the desired questions.

Enabling the subject to talk under hypnosis is especially significant for therapeutic purposes. Through talking with the subject and asking proper therapeutic questions the "imprints" may be abreacted in only two or three sessions. If this was done by traditional methods of psychotherapy it would probably take several months.

To enable the subject to talk under hypnosis, he may be given the following suggestions: "Although you are under the hypnotic trance, you are both able to hear my voice clearly and able to talk to me without awakening. You are able to do this without any difficulty whatsoever— and without coming out of the trance."

Opening the Eyes Without Awakening

The hypnotic subject may be instructed by the hypnotist to open his eyes and remain in his current stage of hypnosis. In the deep stages of hypnosis—with proper suggestions—the subject can open his eyes without coming out of the trance, but in the medium or lighter stages of hypnosis the trance tends to become lighter and the subject may even wake up. However, even when not in a deep trance, it is possible for a subject to open his eyes.

To enable the subject to open his eyes under hypnosis, without coming out of the trance, the following suggestion may be used: "In a moment I am going to count to 'five.' When I reach the count of 'five,' you will be able to open your eyes but will still remain at the very same depth of hypnosis you are in right now. When you open your eyes you will be able to look around, move around, and see clearly everything that I point out."

After the subject opens his eyes, the hypnotist may experiment with hallucination in different ways. For instance, he may ask him to "read the time from the clock on the wall" (when, in fact, no clock is there). The subject will look at the wall and, interestingly, will tell the time with almost complete accuracy. If he is asked about the color of the clock, he will also imagine a color and describe it.

Hallucinations

This test requires the hypnotized person to produce hallucinations, delusions, and illusions. In general, hallucination is a symptom of psychotic disorder, but normal people may also produce hallucination under the influence of hypnotic suggestion. Hallucinations fall into three main categories: positive hallucination, negative hallucination, and mixed hallucination. To hallucinate positively is to perceive objects which do not have physical reality. To hallucinate negatively is to fail to perceive objects which do have physical reality. Mixed hallucination is a combination of positive and negative hallucination.

A delusion is a false belief about things which are real. For instance, if the subject is told that he is a famous actor on his way to a television interview, the hypnotized person will show through his posture, mannerisms, attitudes, and speech clear alterations that are consistent with his delusion.

An illusion, closely related to hallucination, is a perception which fails to give the true character of an object. The only difference between hallucination and illusion is that hallucination—being an imaginary perception—has no external reality, whereas the latter does. If a subject accepts that there is a cat sitting in front of him (when there is no cat present) he is in a state of hallucination. But if there really is a cat in the room and the subject beleives that the cat is a lion, then a state of illusion is produced. In this sense, an illusion may be considered the same as a mixed hallucination.

Hallucinations are usually difficult to produce under hypnosis and negative hallucinations are more difficult to elicit than positive ones. For this reason positive hallucination, in all the scales of hypnotic depth measurement discussed in Chapter 15, ranked before negative hallucination. Hallucination can be induced in all five of the senses. However, not all of the senses are equally apt to produce hallucination. It is the easiest to elicit tactile hallucination (which is why it is favored by stage hypnotists), followed by olfactory and

and gustatory hallucination. The visual hallucinations are the hardest to produce. It also should be pointed out that hallucination is not necessarily restricted to one sense at a time. Two or more senses may be involved simultaneously when each of the senses involved reinforce each other. For instance, if it is suggested to the hypnotized person that a potato is a peach, the hallucination can be reinforced by telling the subject that he can actually smell the odor of a peach.

In hypnosis, the senses become very sensitive to a degree not possible in the waking state. There is no limit to the various kinds of hallucinations that can be suggested. Some examples of these are outlined below: If it is suggested to a subject that his nose is beginning to itch, he will indeed feel an itch and try to scratch. This suggestion may also be given to a subject post-hypnotically (tactile hallucination). A bottle of ammonia may be put under the nose of a deeply hypnotized subject and it be suggested that it is perfume. The subject will inhale the fumes with obvious enjoyment and without the normal reaction to an unpleasant substance (olfactory hallucination). The subject may be given a potato and told that it is a succulent peach. The subject will eat the potato with the physical reactions characteristic of eating a peach (gustatory hallucination). If a deeply hypnotized subject is told that he is listening intently to an orchestra or to an impressive speech, he will produce the same facial gestures and other appropriate reactions as a person in a natural and genuine experience does (auditory hallucination). The subject may be told that when he opens his eyes he will see a kitten sitting on his lap. Upon opening his eyes, the subject will really observe a cat and pet it (visionary hallucination). The subject may be told that he is in a very warm place, such as a desert, and that the heat is unbearable. The subject will show the reaction of a person being scorched by heat. The subject also may be told that he is freezing in a remote place at the North Pole. The subject will produce the reaction of a person shivering in unbearable cold.

Weitzenhoffer[11] states that it is a good idea when producing hallucinations to first inquire about the subject's likes, dislikes, and other relevant idiosyncracies. He adds that a hypnotized subject once promptly fainted when told that a swarm of bees was after her. He was not aware that she was apiphobic (a severe phobia concerning bees).

REFERENCES

1. London, "Subject Characteristics in Hypnosis Research," *International Journal of Clinical and Experimental Hypnosis,* 9:151-61, 1961.
2. Wolberg, *Medical Hypnosis,* 1:157.
3. Hilgard and Cooper, "Spontaneous and Suggested Post-hypnotic Amnesia," *International Journal of Clinical and Experimental Hypnosis,* 13: 261-73.
4. Wolberg, *Medical Hypnosis,* 1:p 55
5. Kroger, *Clinical and Experimental Hypnosis,* p.15.
6. West and Hardy, "Effects of Hypnotic Suggestion on Pain Perception and Galvanic Skin Response," *Archives of Neurology and Psychatry,* 68:549, 1952.
7. Erickson, "The Induction of Color Blindness by a Technique of Hypnotic Suggestion," *Journal of General Psychology,* 20:61-89, 1939.
8. Erickson, "A Study of Clinical and Experimental Findings on Hypnotic Deafness: 1. Clinical Experimentation and Findings," *Journal of General Psychology,* 19:127-50, 1938.
9. Kroger, *Clinical and Experimental Hypnosis,* p.56.
10. Sparks, *Self-Hypnosis: A Conditioned Response Technique* (Wilshire Book Company, 1962), pp. 103-4.
11. Weitzenhoffer, *General Techniques of Hypnotism,* p.358.

CHAPTER SEVENTEEN

SUGGESTION

Suggestion plays a central role in hypnosis and in modern techniques of induction. As already mentioned, some authors have equated suggestion with hypnosis, stating that there is no hypnosis, only suggestion; some believe that no one knows where suggestion ends and hypnosis starts. Whatever the truth, it is obvious that hypnosis is very closely related to suggestion. A suggestion is actually an ideational stimulus. It is the process of uncritical acceptance of an idea for belief or action.

Broadly speaking, in hypnosis parlance, the term "suggestion" is used to describe the ideas the hypnotist puts forward while inducing the hypnotic state, and the instructions he gives to the subject after he is hypnotized (post-hypnotic suggestion). Based on the aforementioned premise and the definitions of other authors, we can say that suggestion is: "a stimulus which implants an idea in another person's mind and initiates alterations of mental processes or of behavior in him, almost voluntarily and automatically."

To understand the mechanism of suggestion, we have to

take into consideration the fact that human nature is inclined to disregard any new idea in favor of one that is familiar. Two conflicting ideas cannot coexist within the mind, one must die for the other to prevail. "It is impossible to experience two opposing thoughts (for example, love and hate) simultaneously without internal conflict."[1]

When a new idea is placed in a person's mind, it can only gain a foothold by displacing an opposing idea which is already present. In the conscious state, this process usually causes much resistance and argument. The mind tends to reject or suppress any new idea attempting to invade it, however practical, valuable, or realistic it might be. In hypnosis, we are able to create a direct pathway to even the most stubborn mind along which the new idea may travel, dissolving the barriers along the way by suggestion. Once the new idea has become acceptable to the subject, his mental and physical faculties all cooperate to carry out the new idea.[2] Because of this, in the preinduction talk the subject should be instructed to make his mind inactive, to be completely passive, and not to think or analyze what is being suggested to him. Over-curiousness and over-cooperativeness cause resistances which block the hypnotic process.

A suggestion is more readily accepted by a subject if there is a sound logical reason for its acceptance. This principle is especially true with waking suggestions. If an illogical suggestion is given to the subject during hypnosis, it may be carried out or possibly rejected, but it will promptly be rejected in the waking state. For instance, to eliminate a pain in some part of the body, it is not appropriate to suggest that the pain has gone; because the person probably still feels it. But if the suggestion is made that the pain will gradually fade away and in a few moments will be entirely eliminated. (Not only will there be time to digest the idea, but it will make more sense; therefore, the suggestion becomes more effective).

Suggestibility increases with greater depths of trance. Therefore, the suggestions given in the deeper stages of trance are more powerful and effective than suggestions given in a lighter trance. In the deeper stages of hypnosis, when the conscious mind is less active and its interference is therefore less, it is easier for the unconscious mind to comply with the suggestion and carry it out. For that very reason, if during a deep trance it is suggested that the subject will forget everything upon awakening—this will indeed occur.

One important aspect of suggestion is that it evokes a non-voluntary response. The subject never initiates the response (the suggested act) consciously. However, the subject may voluntarily initiate subsequent behavior, such as when he reacts to an hallucination, but he has no volitional participation in the first response.

There are a number of different types of suggestions, and they may be categorized as follows: positive and negative, direct and indirect, or permissive and authoritarian. Some types are more effective than others, and some are used for a specific purpose.

Positive suggestions are more effective than negative ones. For example, the phrasing "You will" is more effective than "You won't." By the same token, the phrases "You can't," "You don't" and similar negative phrases, with the implication of "not," should be avoided in suggestions. It has been found that it is 30 per cent more difficult to comprehend a negative idea than a positive one.[3] Negatives can introduce confusion which tends to retard a subject's sense of making progress, and has negative effects on the hypnotized subject.

A direct suggestion is one which is more likely to be weighed, and probably not accepted uncritically by the subject. A direct suggestion appeals to the conscious mind and succeeds in initiating behavior when it is in agreement with the subject and the subject has the ability to carry it out.

An example of direct suggestion is when the operator tells the subject "Close your eyes." Indirect suggestion is more subtle and therefore may escape both conscious and unconscious censorship—giving it a better chance of being immediately accepted and carried out. The indirect form of suggestion does not tell the subject what to do; rather, it explores and facilitates what the subject's response system can do voluntarily. An indirect suggestion automatically initiates unconscious searches independent of the conscious will. For example, an indirect suggestion of eye closure would be, " . . . when a sensation of relaxation spreads to the whole of your body, your eyelids will droop."

Permissive and authoritarian forms of suggestion have already been discussed. The wording of a suggestion may be in a commanding or a permissive manner. Most people are not willing to be ordered to do something by others and, as a result, are more prone to respond to permissive suggestions. There are, however, some people who have dependent personalities and suggestions administered in a commanding manner will work with them more readily than permissive suggestions. Additionally, permissive suggestions are more suitable for waking state and lighter trance states. Authoritarian and direct suggestions are more appropriate when the subject is under trance. The reason for this is that under hypnosis the critical sensor (the conscious mind) is by-passed, and while hypnotized the subject is in a state of increased suggestibility resulting in suggestions immediately reaching the unconscious mind. When a deep trance is produced and reasoning has been inhibited, even the most unusual suggestions may be carried out.

An interesting question then arises. Can a subject, in fact, be made to carry out a suggestion which is against his/her moral code? Experts have had differing views on this. Some believe that a subject under hypnosis, or following post-hypnotic suggestion, will never commit any action, criminal or otherwise, which he would not be willing to do when awake (or after hypnosis through post-hypnotic suggestion). Those who hold to this view believe that there is always an alertness persisting at the back of the hypnotized subject's mind. It has been shown, however, that this self-control can be suppressed. Taking the necessary precautions, hypnotists have been able to make subjects attempt to seize poisonous rattlesnakes. Other hypnotized subjects have thrown acid at the faces of innocent people (who were protected by an invisible glass shield). Soldier/volunteers, in a military setting, were made to commit anti-social acts by post-hypnotic suggestion.[4] Such behaviors, however, are also possible when the subjects are in the waking state.

Other experimenters have proved that a subject cannot be forced to do whatever he does not do when awake, or anything which is against his moral code. Conn[5] has accomplished an extensive study about the possibility of performing an antisocial act by a subject through hypnosis and has reached an emphatic "no answer." However, the rapport and the prestige of the hypnotist plays a great role in the regard.

In the verbalization of suggestions, clarity, simplicity and repetition are very important. The hypnotist should take into consideration that it is not what he thinks and says that is important but what the subject hears and perceives. Repetition of suggestions also makes them more effective. By repeating them, there is more of a chance for the ideas to be impressed on the unconscious mind. At the same time it should be noted that if the unconscious mind is overloaded with more than one idea at a time it will be confused and difficulty may arise in the execution of the suggestion. Therefore, it is advisable to give only one suggestion to the subject at any one session.

There is considerable evidence that the powers of suggestion are based to a large degree upon the prestige of the hypnotist and the way such prestige is perceived by the subject. Some investigators believe that the successful practice of suggestive hypnosis is dependent on the establishment and maintenance of an atmosphere of faith in hypnosis. "Anything that lowers that intensity of faith decreases the strength of suggestion. If the subject doubts the skill and power of the hypnotist, he will probably develop a powerful resistance to hypnosis. Where he accepts on faith the power of the hypnotist, he will respond to suggestions, even those which there are no logical grounds."[6]

There are some important "laws" which should be taken into account when suggestion is given to a subject.

The Law of Reversed Effect

This principle, initiated by Emil Coue,[7] indicates that the expectation of a sensation tends to bring about the realization because imagination is stronger than will power. When the will and the imagination are at war the imagination always wins. The force of imagination is in direct ratio to the square of the will.

According to this law, the harder one tries to do something (using will power) the less one is able to do it. An example given by Coue is that if a board a foot wide is placed on the floor a person will be able to walk its length without having a need even to glance at it. If the same board is placed between two chairs two feet from the floor, it will still be easy to walk its length but with more care. But if the same board is placed between the towers of a cathedral, the person probably could not even start to walk on it, because his imagination overcomes his will. Continually thinking negative and harmful thoughts finally leads to their realization because of the expectation and belief that they will happen. Having an idea of an action often results in that action.

According to this law, the harder one wills oneself to remember a word or a name—or to fall asleep, for that matter—the less chance one has to succeed. This law must be remembered when phrasing a suggestion; suggestions should embody principles of "imagination power" rather than "will power."

The Law of Dominant Effect

The law of dominant effect was developed by Frederick Pierce, a follower of Coue. This law indicates that a strong emotion tends to replace a weaker one. When a person experiences a pleasurable emotion and danger arises, because the danger is stronger, the pleasurable emotion will imediately disappear.

These laws are the basis for the success of different techniques used by hypnotists and hypnotherapists. To achieve a greater result from a suggestion, it should be attached to an emotion which by-passes any other active emotion in the mind. In the hypnotic treatment of smoking, for instance, a feeling of disgust and nausea may be attached to the suggestion of loss of desire to smoke.

The Laws of Precedence

Exploring the ability of the subject to resist non-noxious stimuli, Weitzenhoffer[8] has developed three laws: the law of temporal precedence, the law of depth of precedence, and the law of impressional precedence.

The law of temporal precedence states: "All other things being equal, when two antagonistic suggestions are given, the one that is given first has precedence over the later one." The rationale behind this law is that if two opposing but non-noxious suggestions are given to a subject, the subject will focus his attention on the first suggestion and it will be carried out.

The law of the depth of precedence indicates: "All other things being equal, of two conflicting suggestions, the one associated with the greater trance depth will be carried out."

The law of impressional precedence states: "All other things being equal, of two opposing suggestions, the one impressed most strongly through factors other than trance depth has precedence over the other." By "impressional precedence" Weitzenhoffer means the degree of association between the suggestion and the subject's already existing determinants of behavior.

REFERENCES

1. Gindes, *New Concepts of Hypnosis*, p. 180.
2. *Ibid.*
3. Erickson and Rossi, *Hypnotherapy: An Exploratory Casebook*, p. 35.
4. Watkins, J. G., "Anti-Social Compulsions Induced Under Hypnotic Trance," *Journal of Abnormal Social Psychology*, 42: 256, 1947.
5. Conn, J. H., "Is Hypnosis Really Dangerous?", *International Journal of Clinical and Experimental Hypnosis*, 20: 61-79, 1972.
6. Wolberg, *Medical Hypnosis*, 1:77.
7. Coue, E. *Self-Mastery Through Conscious AutoSuggestion* (New York: American Library Service, 1922), p. 7-8.
8. Weitzenhoffer, A., *Hypnotism: An Objective Study in Susceptibility*, pp. 201-2.

CHAPTER EIGHTEEN

POST-HYPNOTIC SUGGESTION

Post-hypnotic suggestion is one of the most significant phenomena of hypnosis. If it were not due to the post-hypnotic phenomenon, hypnosis would be no more useful than a sleeping pill or a placebo in eliminating a habit. It may be compared with the conditioned reflex even though it is not as rapidly terminated as a conditioned reflex.

A post-hypnotic suggestion is given to the subject while he is hypnotized, but its effect is seen after the subject has been de-hypnotized. Response to the post-hypnotic suggestion is a kind of compulsive behavior, a desire to complete an uncompleted job. The action and the desire to perform it is clear to the subject, but the reason or motivation is unknown. When a subject carries out a post-hypnotic suggestion he usually rationalizes this compulsive behavior, especially if he has no memory (amnesia) of the suggestion's origin. If questioned as to the reason for his unusual behavior, the subject may answer, "I just liked to do it. It seemed to be a nice idea."

Response to post-hypnotic suggestion differs greatly in

many respects. Some subjects will complete each suggestion, others will resist or for some reason fail to comply, while still others may obey one aspect of the suggestion and reject another aspect even though the trance may have been deep.

In 1941 Milton and Elizabeth Erickson published a paper critical of much of the previous research on hypnotic behavior because it concentrated on the outward behavior of the subject rather than on his mental condition at the time of the behavior. In that paper they defined post-hypnotic suggestion as the following: "A post-hypnotic act has been found to be one performed by the hypnotic subject after awakening from a trance, in response to suggestions given during the trance state, with the execution of the act marked by an absence of any demonstrable conscious awareness in the subject of the underlying cause and motive for his act.[1] Regarding the nature of the post-hypnotic state, Milton and Elizabeth Erickson believe that the hypnotic subject instructed to execute some act post-hypnotically, invariably develops hypnotic trance spontaneously, affording a convenient manner of re-hypnotizing himself (and needing no further suggestion or instruction in this regard). In other words, post-hypnotic suggestion constitutes a resurgence of a self-limited hypnosis. This mini-trance state is said to be in no way different from the original trance, is usually of brief duration, and occurs in direct relation to the performance of the post-hypnotic act. This special trance state occurs as readily in the naive as in the highly trained subject: its manifestations differ essentially in no way from those of an ordinarily induced trance.

The post-hypnotic suggestions are believed to be more effective if amnesia is present. However, they can still be quite effective even though no amnesia or any partial amnesia is present. Many people who are resistant to deep trance induction, will cooperate for the development of the spontaneous trance.

Some subjects develop a complete amnesia for the post-hypnotic action and still carry out the suggestion. Others are completely conscious of the post-hypnotic suggestion as they execute it. Still others remember the suggestion only after the completion of the act.[2]

By and large, a greater depth of hypnosis (a score of 15 on the David-Husband scale of hypnotic susceptibility, a score of 30 on the Lecron-Bordeaux scale, and the fourth stage of Aron's depth rule)* is required to develop this particular phenomenon. For the best results, post-hypnotic suggestions should be stated as specifically as possible and repeated several times.

Post-hypnotic suggestion is more effective if a more simple suggestion is given initially and then built up to a higher order of complexity. A post-hypnotic suggestion may lose effectiveness with time, and the extent of loss is directly related to the following factors: the phrasing of the suggestion given to the subject, difficulty or complexity of the suggestion, the subject's depth of hypnosis, the failure to develop amnesia, and the willingness of the subject to perform the suggested act. Periodic reinforcement, however, tends to increase its effectiveness, repeated elicitation does not weaken it. Completion of the post-hypnotic action depends more on the nature and the difficulty of the suggested action rather than upon the depth of the hypnosis.[3] When the suggestion is acceptable the subject finds it very

---

*See Chapter 15.

difficult to reject its execution. Such a suggestion given to a deeply hypnotized subject may last months and even years. For the same reason, unless the subject voluntarily wishes to cooperate with a stage hypnotist, bizarre and ridiculous post-hypnotic suggestions are rejected. These post-hypnotic suggestions are as readily forgotten as other instructions given at waking levels.[4]

Generally speaking, a post-hypnotic suggestion may last from minutes to years.[5] Most researchers however, indicate that it may remain effective for several months.[6] Sheehan and Orne report studies showing effects "lasting in excess of 3 months."[7] Milton and Elizabeth Erickson report the performance of post-hypnotic acts after periods of from months to 4 or 5 years from the hypnotic session.[8]

The mental mechanism by which a subject accepts a post-hypnotic suggestion is that selective cortical inhibition does not permit the incoming information (suggestion), to have access to the stored data in the mind. Therefore, the incoming information can not be evaluated or validated and is accepted as reality. Post-hypnotic suggestion is far more likely to be accomplished if coupled with a certain signal, or if a specific time is set. For example, it is suggested to the subject under hypnosis (of course, repetitively), that upon waking the hypnotist will tap three times on the table and then the subject will feel an irresistible urge to get a drink of water. Or it may be suggested to the subject post-hypnotically that 10 minutes after he wakes up, he will find that one of his feet itches so severely that he will be compelled to take off his shoes. The above post-hypnotic suggestion naturally may be given to the subject without a definite signal or a certain time set.

If the post-hypnotic suggestion tended to inhibit the

subject from performing a particular kind of action temporarily (for instance, striking a match after waking) the suggestion should be properly removed. This can be done with a releasing signal such as a clap of the hands, a cough, a snap of the fingers, or a time limit. The post-hypnotic suggestion, will then die away, but if it is not removed properly, it may cause the subject to feel numbness in certain parts of the body involved in the suggestion and it may also last longer than it normally would.

Post-hypnotic suggestions have many therapeutic benefits. They are the power behind hypnotic influence. Bad habits are replaced by good habits through post-hypnotic suggestion. When good habits are firmly established in this way, they tend to persist indefinitely in the same way as bad habits.

REFERENCES

1. Erickson and Erickson, "Concerning the Nature and Character of Post-Hypnotic Behavior," *Modern Hypnosis,* ed. Kuhn and Russo (Hollywood, California: Wilshire Book Company, 1975), p. 106.
2. Kroger, *Hypnosis and Behavior Modification,* p. 15.
3. Weitzenhoffer, "A Note on the Persistance of Hypnotic Suggestion," *Journal of Abnormal and Social Psychology,* 45:160, 1950.
4. Sears, "A Comparism of Hypnotic and Waking Recall," *Journal of Clinical and Experimental Hypnosis,* 2:296, 1954.
5. Edwards, "Duration of Post-Hypnotic Effect," *British Journal of Psychiatry,* 109:259, 1963.
6. Kellogg, "Duration of the Effects of Post-Hypnotic Suggestion," *Journal of Experimental Psychology,* 12:502, 1929.
7. Udolf, *Handbook of Hypnosis for Professionals,* p.148.
8. Ibid., p.144.

CHAPTER NINETEEN

SIGNS OF HYPNOSIS

The production of hypnosis in subjects is usually accompanied by a number of physiological and psychological signs. Physiological changes during hypnosis are observable; psychological sensations are not—they are only felt by the subject. From the very moment hypnosis takes effect there will be an immediate alteration in bodily functions, particularly in the limbs; and a heightened sensory awareness.

An experienced hypnotist will carefully monitor the physiological changes in the subject and try to match hypnotic induction to those signs and symptoms observed. From these signs the skilled practitioner will be able to identify the varied degrees of the hypnotic trance, and will also be able to assess the responsiveness of the subject to hypnotic suggestion.

Physiological Signs

More than any other part of the body the eyes mirror the stages of hypnosis. When a subject is under hypnotic suggestion the immediate effect is on the eyelids. While the eyes are still open, and even for a few moments after they are closed, the lids frequently involuntarily tremble and flutter. This signals the beginning of the trance and is one of the most common indications of a light trance. The eyes, narrowing to a slit, may become watery and even shed tears before closing. Before this happens, it is best to ask the subject to close his eyes. If the eyelids continue to tremble after the eyes are closed this usually indicates a further deepening of the trance. On rare occasions the eyes will remain open even after the production of a trance, or they will close only partially during which the whites of the eyes are seen. If, during the trance, the eyes remain open they will appear glassy and stare straight ahead. In a deep state, if the subject is told to open his eyes and remain under trance, the eyes will also have a peculiar glassy look and seem to stare fixedly into space. The movement of the eyes under hypnosis becomes very slow or ceases. If the eyes move from side to side it indicates that the subject is about to enter catalepsy. If the eyes roll up into the head, it is a sign that the hypnotic process is progressing too fast and that the subject is on the verge of somnambulism.

Generally, under a hypnotic trance a subject shows signs of complete listlessness or lethargy. Voluntary and involuntary actions become slow or cease. The arms drop limply by their sides; the subject is disinclined to move unless it is suggested that he do so. In the medium or deeper stages of trance, it may be suggested to the subject that his hands slowly turn around each other, moving faster and faster at the hypnotist's command. When the movement of the hands has been speeded up and the arms are twirling around and around each other, it is suggested to the subject that if he tries to stop he will be unable to do so—and the harder he tries to stop, the more quickly the hands will move (See Figure 13). After the test has been successfully carried out, the hypnotist will count to three and tell the subject to stop.

The subject may, under hypnosis, be completely motionless for hours without making the slightest movement, something almost impossible to do voluntarily. Even if the subject becomes discomforted e.g., developing an itch, he will never take the trouble of moving.

With increasing depth of trance, the head falls forward on the subject's chest or on the shoulder which is closest to the hypnotist, as if its weight is unbearable. This is a sign that the subject is sinking into a deeper stage of the hypnotic trance. When this occurs, some subjects suffer from straining of the neck muscles. If necessary the hypnotist should support the head of the subject in the most comfortable position.

Figure 13

As the subject drifts into a deeper trance, his face becomes completely expressionless and his jaw becomes totally limp. The subject is disinclined to talk spontaneously. If he is asked a question he will pause before he responds. When this happens the hypnotist should motivate him to talk, and when the subject does speak, it will usually be in a slurred, slow, and effortless fashion.

Under hypnosis the perception of the subject becomes literal and somewhat childlike because, as has already been discussed, the unconscious mind—with all its peculiarities—will take over the conscious mind. Therefore, the suggestions should be worded carefully. Puns and idioms should be avoided, and if necessary, the suggestions should be repeated in different words to make sure that the subject assimilates the suggestions as intended.

One of the most obvious signs of the hypnotic trance is excessive salivation and swallowing. The rate of breathing, and the heartbeat rate, will also change. At the beginning of the induction, however, some subjects may have a temporary increase in hearbeat and breathing due to tension or anxiety associated with hypnosis and its induction. As the trance progresses these subjects experience a gradual slowing of the heartbeat and breathing rates to normal and below normal rates. In the lighter stages of hypnosis breathing is usually diaphragmatic; in the deeper stages, however, the breathing becomes more abdominal. Shaffer and Dorcus[1] have found that the pulse will slow down and the blood pressure decrease.

The above-mentioned physiological signs of hypnosis, though common, are highly individual and vary with different subjects. A subject in a light stage of hypnosis may manifest all or most of them, while another subject under a

deep trance may not show any of them. However, throughout the hypnotic session, the hypnotist should try to pay
close attention to the hypnotic signs and all the various
aspects of the subject's behavior. The information that the
hypnotist obtains through these signs will enable him to
deepen the trance and follow a successful hypnotic process.
The more the hypnotist is observant and alert to the hypnotic signs, the more successful he will be in helping the
subject accomplish induction of hypnosis.

Psychological Signs

The psychological sensations a subject experiences are
generally soothing and pleasant—and include one or more
of the following: (1) a disinclination to move spontaneously
or to apply any kind of effort, (2) feelings of peacefulness
and calmness, (3) sensations of heaviness especially in the
limbs, (4) sensations of numbness and tingling over the whole
body especially in the limbs, (5) feelings of being relieved,
being brighter, and having far greater command of the senses
than in the waking state, (6) sensations of lightness—as though
floating in the air, (7) sensations of detachment as though the
subject has left his body, (8) underestimating the time. Because hypnotic relaxation is pleasant and soothing, time for
the subject will be shortened. For instance, a subject under
hypnosis for approximately an hour, when asked how long
he was under trance, usually answers that it took only 15
minutes or so, (9) a disinclination to be awakened from the
pleasant feelings experienced during hypnosis.

Most people, before they go under trance, consider themselves unhypnotizable. This is probably because we all underestimate the power of the mind. By the same token, when

a person first experiences the hypnotic trance, he tends to underestimate the depth of hypnosis and seldom will accept the fact that he was hypnotized. After he is awakened the hypnotist usually hears something like this: "I don't believe I was hypnotized, I was just relaxed; I was aware of everything and in full control of myself." This is a common reaction after experiencing light and medium stages of hypnosis for the first time, and occurs because most people expect to be "knocked out." Naturally, hypnotic depth tests such as eye catalepsy, limb catalepsy, etc. will make him believe that he was really hypnotized.

REFERENCES

1. Shaffer, G. W. and R. Dorcus. *Textbook of Abnormal Psychology* (Baltimore: Williams & Wilkins, 1939).

CHAPTER TWENTY

DE-HYPNOTIZATION

De-hypnosis or the awakening of the subject is usually one of the simplest parts of hypnosis. The awakening of the subject can be performed by simply suggesting to him that he is to open his eyes and be wide awake. The hypnotist may also order the subject gently to wake up, or he might tell the subject that on a given signal such as a clap of the hands or a snap of the fingers, that he will be wide awake.

The termination of the trance should always be accompanied by suitable suggestions indicative of good health, good thoughts and general well being. Upon waking, the subject should be made to feel happy, cheerful and normal in every way. Otherwise, he may get headaches, eye-strain, grogginess or other discomforts after awakening.

De-hypnotization may be compared with awakening from natural sleep. As the sound sleepers tend to wake up slowly, so the subjects who have been in a deep trance also will be de-hypnotized more slowly than those who have been under a lighter trance. Therefore, the above mentioned methods may be considered suitable for waking subjects who have been in a light trance, but will be somewhat unpleasant for those subjects who have been under the last stages of a medium or deep trance. For the latter group it is better to make the procedure gentle and gradual. A good way of de-hypnotizing those subjects who have been in a deep trance is to count to 3 or 5 and instruct the subject that as the hypnotist counts, the subject will begin to wake gradually and by the number designated, he will open his eyes and be completely awake. A very common reaction of the subject upon waking is to stretch.

If a subject is left to himself without being de-hypnotized, he will usually wake up of his own accord after at most a few hours. No one has ever stayed in hypnosis for a long period of time. If nothing at all was done to facilitate awakening, the person probably would soon drop off into natural sleep and eventually would wake up on his own.[1] "Individuals who have been hypnotized and then left alone, tend to awaken spontaneously within twelve hours (the time seems to be a function of the individual rather than of the hypnotist).[2]

Very rarely, however, a subject may be encountered who refuses to wake in the process of de-hypnotization. This situation is indeed rare but can occur. If a subject does not awaken immediately upon the suggestion to do so, there is always some reason for it. The causes of resistance to de-hypnotization may be one of the following: (1) the subject's hostility toward the hypnotist (2) the subject may be trying to test the ability of the hypnotist to awaken him[3] (3) the subject is not willing to carry out a certain post-hypnotic suggestion (4) the subject is not willing to relinquish the pleasant and relaxing condition of the trance (5) the subject has a difficult life situation to face and therefore he would rather remain in hypnosis (6) some subjects are only partially de-hypnotized and then can lapse into deep hypnosis spontaneously.[4] (7) hypnosis may have converted into fugue.* (A very rare incident).

If a subject rejects de-hypnotization, without showing loss of self-assurance, and using his judgement, the hypnotist should try one of these approaches to rouse him (1) ask the subject why he won't wake up (2) tell the subject that if he will not wake up, he will be left alone (however, the subject should be taken care of until he is thoroughly awake) (3) blow sharply on the closed eyes of the subject (4) the subject's eyelids may be raised and short sharp breaths blown into his eyes (5) a small fan may be placed in front of the subject, his eyelids raised and cool air allowed to hit his face and his eyes (6) tell the subject that because of his unwillingness to wake up, his face will be washed with a cold towel (7) the subject may be exposed to a cold draft of air.

Upon waking, the subject should never be allowed to leave the premise until his condition is properly checked and assurance is obtained that he is wide awake and that he is completely able to control himself.

---

*Fugue is a long period (days, weeks, or even years), in which a patient has almost complete amnesia for his past, although habits and skills are usually little affected. The person leaves home and starts a new life, with sharply different modes of conduct. Upon recovery, there is complete restoration of pre-fugue memory but those of the period of fugue are forgotten. The state of fugue arises out of an unconscious desire to escape a threatening or intensely distasteful life situation.

REFERENCES

1. Cheek and LeCron, *Clinical Hypnotherapy,* p. 71.
2. Marcuse, *Hypnosis: Fact and Fiction,* p. 168.
3. Williams, "Difficulty in De-Hypnotizing," *Journal of Clinical and Experimental Psychology,* 1:3-12, 1953.
4. *Ibid.*

CHAPTER TWENTY ONE

PHENOMENA OF HYPNOSIS

Rapport

The term rapport refers to a close harmonious relationship between the subject and the hypnotist. Rapport is one of the most significant factors in producing a successful hypnotic state. It is a positive feeling of understanding and mutual regard between agent and subject. Rapport is a tool by which the agent secures the attention and cooperation of the subject for a successful hypnotic induction. Some experimenters such as Hull[1] and Young[2,3] maintain that hypnotic rapport is not a spontaneous phenomenon but develops during hypnosis so that the subject only responds to the hypnotist.

The notion that the subject disregards everybody except the hypnotist and follows only the suggestions of the hypnotist unless the rapport is transferred to someone else (and the subject is instructed by the hypnotist to switch his attention to another) has been generally rejected. It appears that the responsiveness of the subject to the hypnotist or to anybody else depends on his attitude and desires. In line with this idea, Moll[4] divides rapport into "isolated rapport" and "plain rapport." Isolated rapport is when the subject responds only to the hypnotist and "plain rapport" is when the subject responds most strongly to the hypnotist but may still respond more weakly to others.

Almost all of the investigators including Erickson have come to the conclusion that rapport is a specific requirement for a successful trance induction, and is part of the hypnotic state. When rapport is established between the subject and the agent, the hypnotic process develops more rapidly along the following lines: (1) greater attention is paid to the agent by the subject, (2) suggestions from the agent are more readily followed, (3) the subject tends to eliminate all the environmental stimuli except the hypnotist, and (4) the prestige of the hypnotist causes the enhancement of rapport and this in turn expedites the hypnotic trance.

Time Distortion

Time distortion, one of the most interesting phenomena of hypnosis, refers to the ability of the human mind to estimate, contract, or expand time. At non-hypnotic levels too, when we are involved in a tedious situation (for instance, watching a boring movie), the time will expand and one minute seems like ten minutes. Conversely, when we are involved in a pleasant activity (for instance, listening to an interesting lecture), the time will contract and one minute passes as if it were twenty minutes.

Under hypnosis, the propensity of man to distort time, is increased through suggestion. During hypnosis, good subjects have stated that suggestions of time distortion have been effective in altering their perception of time and that the passage of time has been speeded up or slowed down greatly for them.

Cooper and Erickson[5] suggested to deeply hypnotized subjects that time would pass slowly, and seconds seem like minutes or hours. They were given only several seconds to perform some tasks. Following the experiment, the subjects reported that time passed slower for them and they were able to execute complex things in a single second. For example, a hypnotized subject may be able to experience a full-length motion-picture film in only a few seconds. Of course, the speeding up of the brain during hypnosis is contingent upon proper suggestions on the part of the hypnotist. There are various types of suggestions which distort objective time into subjective time. A hypnotized subject may be told that he will continue a certain activity for a given length of subjective time, he may be told to engage in an activity without a suggestive time limit and to discontinue it whenever he wishes. The degree to which time distortion can be produced often depends on the depth of hypnotic trance. Relevant research, however, has proven that such subjective time distortion during hypnosis can not objectively accelerate the learning process of new information.

The phenomenon of time distortion has many advantages for therapeutic purposes. For a patient who is suffering from pain, hours may be made to seem like minutes or even seconds. The psychiatrist or hypnotherapist may be able to expand or contract the subjective time of the patient in order to enable the patient to review his past much more rapidly than any other method.

Dissociation

Dissociation is a particular aspect of the hypnotic state in which the subject is segregated from his immediate environment. Dissociation theory was formulated by Pierre Janet[6] and supported by Prince,[7] Brunett[8] and Sidis.[9] These prominent psychological authorities believed that in hypnosis intellectual processes could be split off from each other—functioning simultaneously and separately by suggestion. One of the ramifications of this theory is that the hypnotized individual becomes dissociated or split off from his conscious awareness and his unconscious mind takes over. This theory, although popular at one time, fell into disrepute because, if taken as a valid theory, amnesia would always occur spontaneously and could not be removed by suggestion. Furthermore, we know that during hypnosis hyperaesthesia (hypersensitivity) is usually produced rather than amnesia or dissociation. In brief, although some degree of dissociation develops when amnesia is present, this does not mean that dissociation brings about a hypnotic trance or resembles it.

This phenomenon also occurs in deep hypnosis and it somewhat resembles hypnotic amnesia. It seems that in the dissociative state the subject excludes all environmental consciousness except the hypnotist as a source of stimulation. Kubie and Margolin[10] have interpreted dissociation as an extension of the ego of the subject into that of the hypnotist.

Dissociation is sometimes used to produce hypnoanaesthesia, and "depersonalization" is also developed as a type of dissociation. In deeper states of hypnosis the subject is told to forget his identity and assume the personality characteristics of an individual whom he wishes to be. The tendency to dissociate can be enhanced through suggestion, but this does not necessarily mean that hypnosis and dissociation are the same thing.

Age Regression

One of the most interesting and at the same time controversial phenomena of hypnosis is age regression. This can be defined as an actual organic reproduction of an earlier period of life.[11] In regression the subject withdraws into himself and tries to re-create the world of his past. The personality of the regressed subject will be changed and he will think and behave as he did at that time.

The most interesting research into age regression has been carried out by Erickson and Kubie. [12] They state that there are two ways to regress the hypnotic subject to an earlier period of his life. The first type they label "age regression." With age regression, the subject behaves in a way that he, as an adult, believes would be suitable for him as a child at the suggested age level; in other words, he understands his regressed-age incidents with his adult viewpoint. The subject is half-conscious and aware of where he is—and he knows the identity of the hypnotist.

The second type of regression, a true regression, is called "revivification," and is far different in character from "age regression." In revivification, it is suggested to the subject that he is a certain age, or has returned to a specific age or experience. Age regression is actually a return to any particular age suggested by the hypnotist, even to a certain date in the subject's life. The regression may even be directed to a special day, such as a birthday or Christmas, or Easter, or other holiday, etc. The specific time of the occasion is also important. The subject is told that he will feel exactly as he did in that situation—he will see the same things and persons he saw then, etc.

When the age of the subject is turned back to childhood, his way of thinking and his behavior become that of the suggested age. The present time, and all subsequent life experiences after that age, become blotted out. The subject's voice and handwriting become childlike. Some even become non-verbal when regressed to the age of six months. The "mental" age of the regressed subject will tally with the chronological age he has been regressed to. [13] If the subject is given an intelligence quotient, or other psychological tests at a certain age during regression, the result will indicate the approximate age level to which the subject has returned.[14] The subject may even fail to recognize the hypnotist and may lose rapport with him. LeCron states that in a personal communication Erickson told him that he had regressed a 30 year-old male subject to an infantile level with the intention of studying his behavior at a regressed level. A reaction quite unexpected and embarrassing to both Erickson and the subject was an accompanying urination which soaked the subject's trousers.[15]

In subjects regressed to less than five months of age, there is normally a positive Babinski reflex to stimulation of the sole of the foot. Babinski reflex naturally replaces the plantar reflex during age regression.

With revivification, the hypnotist becomes a stranger to the subject, making both conversation and rapport more difficult. This problem is solved by transforming the hypnotist into someone known to the subject during the earlier period. It is done by suggesting that the operator is someone whom he knows, likes, and trusts—such as a teacher, relative, neighbor, etc.

Although it has been claimed that age regression is even possible to prenatal and neonatal periods, it is not easy to say how far back in a person's life regression may be developed. It certainly varies with the personality make-up of the subject. It probably can be likened to the recall of past memories of the individual.

Age regression is the most valuable tool for therapeutic purposes. To treat a psychogenic or psychosomatic problem, the person is returned to a period before the problem occurred. Gradually he is reoriented to his present age while the development of the illness is discussed. A deep trance state is necessary to produce age regression (a score of 21 on the Davis-Husband scale, a score of 42 on the LeCron-Bordeaux scale, and the fourth stage of Arons' scale). For the purpose of producing regression and revivification, it is best to devote at least two hours to it at any one session. Often a silence period of from ten to fifteen minutes helps to deepen hypnosis provided that the subject is not disturbed during that period.

It has been generally accepted that the powers of memory can be greatly enhanced in hypnosis—particularly during regression.[16] The hypermnesic characteristics of a successful hypnotic age regression (in indicated cases) greatly aids in recovery from emotional problems resulting from forgotten traumatic incidents. It should be carefully noted, however, that the recall of past traumatic events, and the resulting discharge of emotion (catharsis), may put the subject into a critical situation, If the hypnotist is not a clinical psychologist or psychiatrist, or is inexperienced in dealing with the emotionally disturbed subject, a potentially dangerous situation exists.

There are several methods for producing regression. One of the most effective, developed by Erickson, is a combination of disorientation and reorientation. The subject is gradually disoriented with regard to time and place, then he is gradually reoriented. The procedure is carried out by the application of the "confusion technique." At first, confusion is suggested in regard to the exact day or week, then the month, then the year. It is suggested to the subject that he finds it very difficult to remember the day, date, etc., that he is confused about, etc. Further, it is suggested that sometimes a person becomes easily confused as to the day of the week, and can mix up appointments; or give the date of the old year instead of the new year. Under this blanket of confusion the subject becomes extremely receptive to any suggestion which gives him a concrete point of reference. The orientation phase, which takes the subject back to earlier and earlier periods of his life through appropriate suggestion, accomplishes this. If the hypnotherapist does not know at what age the traumatic experience(s) happened, the suggestions should be so administered as to lead the subject to a crucial period. When the subject shows signs of regression, it is suggested to him that he have certain thoughts on his mind which he has never forgotten and he is now able to recall and explain them. This can be done by a signal (counting from 1 to 5, for example).[17]

Both the orientation and reorientation should be employed gradually—step-by-step. At first, the suggestions should be worded in a conversational manner, as thought provoking comments, without any implications of command or instruction. After the subject begins to cooperate and comply with the hypnotist, the suggestions are given in a direct fashion.

A rather simple technique for inducing regression in good subjects, developed by Wolberg,[18] is the use of suggestions in descending order of simplicity. According to this technique, after the subject is deeply hypnotized, the operator gives the following suggestion to the subject:

Now concentrate carefully on what I have to say to you. I am going to suggest that you go back in time, back into the past. You will feel as if you were back in the periods that I suggest to you. Let us start with yesterday. What did you do yesterday morning? What did you have for breakfast? For lunch? Now we are going back to the first day you came to see me. Can you see yourself talking to me? How did you feel? Describe it. What clothes did you wear? Now listen carefully. We are going back to a period when you were little. You are getting small. You are getting smaller and smaller. I am someone you know and like. You are between the ages ten and twelve. Can you see yourself? Describe what you see. Now you are getting even smaller. You are becoming very, very little. Your arms and legs are shrinking. Your body is shrinking. You are going back to a time when you were very, very little. Now you are a very little child. You are going back to the time when you entered school for the first time. Can you see yourself? Who is your teacher? How old are you? What are your friend's names? Now you are even smaller than that; you are much, much smaller. Your mother is holding you. Do you see yourself with your mother? What is she wearing? What is she saying?

If a subject has a particular symptom, such as a phobia, states Wolberg, he may be given a suggestion as follows:

"Now listen carefully. We are going back in time when you first were afraid. What frightened you? Tell me all the details."

Regression increases the hypermnesic effect of hypnosis, opening up channels to forgotten memories and experiences which the person does not usually have access to when awake; it is also a very useful method for the recovery of lost articles (mislaid jewelry, etc.). Additionally, it has been used in criminal investigation to "gain forgotten information from witnesses of some crime, such as the license number of a car used by criminals."[19]

Memory Recall or Hypermnesia

Hypermnesia or memory recall (the opposite of amnesia) is dramatically increased when hypnotized and it is one of the most remarkable of hypnotic phenomena. In general, everything that happens to us is stored in our memory in detail, and we know that the memory is a part of our unconscious mind. All of the incidents that occur to us are mentally recorded, but only the more important of them are subject to recall. The process of memory recall is carried out at will or by a stimulus such as an association of ideas. When we make a conscious effort to remember, the unconscious mind continues the search on its own accord even when the conscious mind has abandoned the effort. Sternberg [20] has found that an unconscious search continues at the rate of approximately thirty items per second even after the conscious mind has become occupied with other matters.

Now considering that hypnosis provides a means of reaching the unconscious mind, it follows that under hypnosis a subject can recall memories completely forgotten and not accessible to the conscious mind. The hypermnesic effect of hypnosis has long been known by investigators. Stalankar and Riddle[21] have found out that recall under hypnosis is 65 per cent greater than at non-hypnotic levels.

There are different kinds of memory loss including ordinary forgetting, the amnesias,* and abnormal forgetting. The latter involves undesirable memories or emotions that have been pushed from the consciousness deliberately because of the discomfort that their recollection would cause the patient or subject. Hypermnesia increases the recall of this kind of material because of its ability to lower the anxiety associated with it, through relaxation and heightened self-confidence. The subject, however, may be influenced by false information and misremember or fabricate material he believes he recalls. Freud, nonetheless, believed that such inaccurate memories were as important as real events because the subject responded to them as though they were true. Like amnesia, hypermnesia may be induced or produced spontaneously.

Hypermnesia should be differentiated from age regression. The former is obtained by suggestion and may not include unimportant minor details; the latter can bring out completely forgotten memories and is an actual reliving of an event at the time at which it happened. The construction of the patter in hypermnesia is in the past tense, while in age regression the questions will be asked in the present tense. In hypermnesia the patient or the subject will recall an incident, but will have forgotten the emotion associated with it; in age regression the full emotion associated with the

---

*Loss of memory due usually to brain injury, shock, fatigue, repression, or illness.

incident will be developed in the patient.

Wolberg [22] states that the application of techniques for hypermnesia depends upon the strength of the patient's repressions. He believes that there are some individuals who do remarkably well with simple suggestions such as, "when I put my hand on your forehead you will relive the experience that you had at the time when you first developed your symptom." Wolberg adds that specific symptoms or time periods may be mentioned. When the subject becomes resistant, direct recall may be reinforced by indirect techniques. He may be told that at the count of five there will appear in his mind a number that represents the number of the letters in the name of the thing he has forgotten. Then he is urged to mention whatever letter comes to his mind at the count of five and the subject will name in jumbled order the forgotten word.

Memory recall is used in criminal investigation for recall of pertinent information that helps solve criminal cases. The Chowchilla kidnapping case is one important example of how hypnosis has been successfully used to provide leads in a criminal investigation:

> In July 1976, 26 children and their bus driver were abducted at gunpoint by masked men driving vans. The frightened prisoners, some hysterical, were taken in the vans to a quarry where they were sealed in an underground tomb. Eventually the driver and two of the boys managed to dig their way out. Later, when the bus driver was questioned, he was unable to remember two of the license plate numbers, although he had tried to memorize them. The FBI suggested hypnosis. The driver agreed. He was successfully hypnotized and brought back to the afternoon of the abduction via the TV screen approach. He suddenly called out two license plate numbers, one of which, except for a single digit, matched a van driven by the kidnappers. This information led agents to the kidnappers, who were convicted and sentenced to life. [23]

Automatic Writing

Automatic writing is an effective way of obtaining access to the unconscious mind—and unearthing causes, conflicts, and motives behind psychological problems (imprints)— which are not available to the conscious mind. When we consider that according to psychological investigations, [24] graphic activity is less inhibited by cerebral control than hypnotic verbalization of feelings and impulses, this method of psychic exploration is especially useful for those who cannot fully express themselves.

In automatic writing, the subject may not be aware of what is being written until it is brought to his conscious consideration later. While writing, the subject may be reading or conversing intelligently on an entirely different subject. On the basis of this fact, it can be argued that the phenomenon of automatic writing is really that of dissociation.

The handwriting of the subject, when automatic writing is elicited during hypnosis, is entirely different than normal. It is, in reality, a form of doodling—the script is childish, the words usually run together, it is difficult to read but still intelligible. In some cases, for the best results automatic writing may be combined with age regression.

Before engaging in automatic writing, the subject is instructed that his hand is dissociated from his body and will write even when engaged in conversation, and that he will have no knowledge of what is being written by the dissociated hand.

Wolberg [25] has described this phenomenon at length, and in a scholarly manner explains a very interesting technique for producing it. He states that the analyst may give the following suggestions under hypnosis to the subject:

As you sit here you will continue to be fast asleep. The arm and hand with which you write will now begin to experience a peculiar sensation. They will feel as though they are no longer a part of you. They will feel comfortable but detached. I am going to place a pencil in your hand, and as soon as I do this you will begin to write as if your hand were moving along without any effort or concentration on your part. Your hand will move along as if it were pushed by some force from the outside. As your hand moves along, you will not be aware of what it is writing.

A pencil is then placed in the subject's hand to engage in writing. If the subject is in a deep trance, he may be instructed to open his eyes and continue writing, though the open eyes pay no attention to what the hand is writing. If the subject is not able to open his eyes without awakening, he may be engaged in conversation while his hand is writing.

It is better that the subject himself be asked to interpret his script under hypnosis. For this purpose, while in hypnosis the subject is told to open his eyes without awakening and interpret his own writing. The subject may also be given a post-hypnotic suggestion to the effect that upon awakening he will be able to interpret his script clearly and completely. If the subject's writing has revealed traumatic material, then amnesia can be produced to protect him from being overwhelmed by traumatic emotions after de-hypnotization.

Hyperesthesia

Hyperesthesia or hypersensitivity refers to the increased sensitivity to sensory ability of a subject under hypnotic

trance. Hyperesthesia is one of the most controversial phenomena of hypnosis. It is the opposite of anaesthesia. In
anaesthesia we inhibit the different senses, but in hyperesthesia we make them super-sensitive.

Marcuse maintains that "a great reserve of potential
exists in many of our senses."[26] This reserve is not used
when it is not needed; however, if required during hypnosis,
it may be elicited.

Hyperesthesia can be produced in all the senses. On suggestion, a subject may be made to manifest acute sensitivity to stimuli enabling him to distinguish variations in
texture and temperature that could not be differentiated
in non-hypnotic levels.[27]

Wolberg[28] states that cutaneous hypersthesia is easier
to induce than anaesthesia and recommends that hyperesthesia be applied before anaesthesia. If hyperesthesia is
applied successfully to the subject, the hypnotist will use
the hypersensitive part of the subject's body as reference
when asking him to differentiate between his hypersensitive and anaesthetic parts. If the subject is able to produce
a certain degree of anaesthesia, it will be increased by a
comparison with the hypersensitive part of the body. If the
subject does not, or develops very little anaesthesia, he
may be guided to sense some hyperesthesia - otherwise he
may not develop any anaesthesia at all.

Hyperesthesia, according to Wolberg, can be produced
by giving the following suggestion to the subject:

*Imagine that you are walking down a corridor and you
notice in the far end corner of the corridor a pail of hot
water. You realize it is hot because the steam issues from the
surface of the water ... Now you become curious about how*

hot the water is, so you walk over to the pail of water, take your right hand and you plunge it into the water. As you plunge it into the water, you feel the heat and pain in your hand. Let yourself go. As soon as you feel a sensation, your left hand will rise about six inches to indicate this state. It rises, and now it comes down. Good. Now I am going to touch your right hand with a pin. You will notice that the hand has become so tender that when I touch it with a pin, it will be as though I am poking a nail through it . . . I am going to touch it with a pin now. It will feel as though I am poking a nail through it . . . You will notice the difference when I touch this tender hand here, and when I touch the other hand with a pin. I will touch the other hand first, and now I am going to touch the tender hand here, this way. Do you notice the difference when I poke it? (patient nods)

Following production of successful hyperesthesia, anaesthesia may be induced.

Dream Induction

A hypnotically induced dream results from a suggestion either during the hypnotic session itself or subsequent to it. When the patient enters spontaneous sleep encouraged by a post-hypnotic suggestion, hypnotically induced dreams and their interpretation play a great role in both hypno-analysis and psychoanalysis because dreams disclose repressed unconscious impulses and memories representing significant psychological traits of the dreamer. During hypnoanalysis or psychoanalysis the study of the patient's dreams disclose the imprints of the patient and his repressed unconscious drives. Dream induction is a valuable tool for cases in which regression and abreaction have not been successful.[29] The hypnotist suggests to the subject during hypnosis that he can dream, even in a specific theme, and remember it upon awakening. When the subject is dreaming during hypnosis, he may be asked to describe it as he is experiencing it.

Farber and Fisher [30] discovered that individuals who were unable to interpret dreams under normal conditions were able to do so when hypnotized. They also discovered that while uninhibited individuals, when hypnotized, could interpret the dreams of others; they were unable to perform this task in the waking state. Some experimenters assert that interpretation of dreams by the dreamer himself during hypnosis is more reliable than in the waking state because the symbolic meanings of the dreams (during hypnosis) are more in evidence for the dreamer than in the waking state.

According to Barber, recent studies suggest that post-hypnotic dreams may be purposely constructed by the subject when he is awake at night, and by what he perceives to be the hypnotist's expectations of him. Barber[31] also maintains that some dreams occurring during the night following the trance may be influenced by a significant event from the preceding day—namely, the hypnotic session itself—in the same way that nocturnal dreams are instigated by the incidents of the day. [32]

Wolberg [33] believes that a medium or deep trance is usually required for dream induction and that it is best to proceed slowly in the dream induction process. At first the subject may be given a post-hypnotic suggestion that in his nocturnal sleep he will have a dream that he will remember. Then the hypnotist suggests a specific topic to dream about. Next, the subject is told that he will have a dream immediately before awakening. Finally, he is instructed to dream during hypnosis and to describe its contents without awakening.*

---

*For more details about dream induction, consult C. Scott Moss, *The Hypnotic Investigation of Dreams* (New York: John Wiley & Sons, Inc., 1967).

REFERENCES

1. Hull, *Hypnosis and Suggestibility*, p. 388.
2. Young, P. C., "Hypnotism," *Psychological Bulletin*, 23:504-23, 1926.
3. _____, "Is Rapport an Essential Characteristic of Hypnosis?," *Journal of Abnormal and Social Psychology*, 22:130-39, 1927.
4. "Der Rapport in der Hypnose. Untersuchungen "Uber den thierischen Magnetismus," Schriften d. ges. F. Psychol. Forsch. I, quoted in Andre Weitzenhoffer, *General Techniques of Hypnotism*, pp. 49-50.
5. Cooper, L. and M. Erickson, *Time Distortion in Hypnosis* (Baltimore: The Williams & Wilkins Co., 1954), Chap. 18 and 19.
6. Janet, P. *Principles of Psychotherapy*, pp. 131-33.
7. _____, "Experiments to Determine Co-conscious (Subconscious) Ideation, " *Journal of Abnormal and Social Psychology*, 3:37,1909.
8. Burnett, C. T., "Splitting the Mind," *Psychological Monograph*, 34:No. 2, 1925.
9. Sidis, B., *Psychopathological Researches* (New York: G. E. Stechert, 1920), pp. 91, 202, 204.
10. Kubie, L. S. and S. Margolin, "The Process of Hypnotism and the Nature of the Hypnotic State, " *Amer. Journal of Psychiatry*, 100: 611-22, 1944.
11. Estabrooks, *Hypnotism.* p. 65.
12. Erickson and Kubie, "The Successful Treatment of a Case of Acute Hysterical Depression by a Return under Hypnosis to a Critical Phase of Childhood," *Psychoanalytic Quarterly*, 10:592, 1941.
13. Pattie, F. A., "The Genuineness of Some Hypnotic Phenomena," in *Hypnosis and its Therapeutic Applications*, ed. R. Dorcus (New York: McGraw-Hill Book Co., Inc.), p. 618.
14. Platonov, I., "On the Objective Proof of the Experimental Personality Age Regression," *Journal of General Psychology*, 9:190-202, 1933.
15. LeCron, ed., *Experimental Hypnosis*.
16. Gibson, H., *Hypnosis: Its Nature & Therapeutic Uses* (New York: Taplinger Pub. Co., 1978), p. 102.
17. Wolberg, L., *Hypnoanalysis* (New York: Grune & Stratton, Inc., 1964), p. 294.

18. *Ibid.,* pp. 294-95.
19. Cheek and Lecron, *Clinical Hypnotherapy,* p. 53.
20. Sternberg, S., "Memory Scanning: New Findings and Current Controversies," *Quarterly Journal of Experimental Psychology,* 22: 1-23, 1975.
21. Stainaker, J. and E. F. Riddle, "The Effect of Hypnosis on Long Delayed Recall," *Journal of General Psychology,* 6:429-40,1932.
22. Wolberg, *Hypnoanalysis,* pp. 328-29.
23. Feldman, S., "Hypnosis: Look Me in the Eyes and Tell Me that is Admissible," *Barrister,* Spring, 1981, p. 4.
24. Wolberg, *Hypnoanalysis,* p. 276.
25. *Ibid.,* pp. 276-81.
26. Marcuse, *Hypnosis: Fact and Fiction,* p. 98.
27. Wolberg, *Medical Hypnosis,* p. 34.
28. *Ibid.,* pp. 131-32.
29. Kroger, *Clinical and Experimental Hypnosis,* p. 375.
30. Farber and Fisher, "An Experimental Approach to Dream Psychology through the Use of Hypnosis," *Psychoanalytic Quarterly,* 12:202-16, 1943.
31. Barber, T. X., "Toward a Theory of 'Hypnotic' Behavior: The 'Hypnotically Induced Dream,' in The *Hypnotic Investigation of Dreams* (New York: John Wiley and Sons, Inc., 1967), p. 229.
32. Wolberg, *Hypnoanalysis,* p. 267.
33. *Ibid.,* p. 227.

CHAPTER TWENTY TWO

DANGERS OF HYPNOSIS

There is considerable evidence indicating that hypnosis per se is not dangerous. In fact, it is probably the most pleasant, relaxing, and least dangerous method of therapy. If there is any danger in hypnosis it lies in its misuse or the mismanagement of the subject—before, after, and particularly during induction procedure. This is why it is foolish to be a subject for a stage hypnotist or for anyone who is not fully competent.

Weitzenhoffer believes that hypnosis is no more dangerous than natural sleep.[1] The great French psychiatrist, Pierre Janet (1859-1947) once said: "The only danger to hypnosis is that it is not dangerous enough."[2] Erickson has also stated that hypnosis itself has never been harmful in any way to a subject, but that like drugs or any other treatment, it can be misused. It is misuse, not hypnosis itself, which could be harmful.[3]

Neglect of Suggestion Removal—One of the dangers of hypnosis, though probably quite rare, is the hypnotist's failure to remove suggestions (hallucination, illusion, delusion, amnesia, anaesthesia, etc.) before awakening and dismissing the subject.

Absence of Post-Hypnotic Sign—If a subject does not carry out a post-hypnotic suggestion, the hypnotist may incorrectly assume that the subject was not hypnotized at all, and, as a result, neglects to remove the suggestion.

Ignorance of the Physical Effects—This danger explained by Marcuse is that the hypnotist ignores the fact that the subject responds physiologically as well as psychologically to suggestion. A subject with a "weak" heart may be told, for example, that he is hanging by a rope some 10,000 feet over a chasm, that his strength is gradually receding, and that he is about to hurtle down onto the rocks below. In reality, the subject may fall from a chair on the floor some 18 inches away. But here the important thing is that the subject responds to the suggestion that he is falling some 10,000 feet, not to the reality of falling 18 inches.[4] (Although Marcuse' example is an extreme one, and one wonders why any operator would give such a bizarre suggestion in the first place, the competent professional should, nevertheless, be aware of the physical and psychological make-up of his subject and word any suggestions to him with that make-up in mind).

Age Regression

Although age regression is one of the most remarkable phenomena of hypnosis, it would be difficult and somewhat dangerous for an unqualified hypnotist to handle emotional disturbances which may be aroused as a result of it. Weitzenhoffer has stated: "I believe that, without exaggeration, every regression experiment should be labeled

'Danger—Potential High Tension.' Regressions are probably the most dangerous of all hypnotic phenomena; one usually does not know what sort of traumatic experiences the subject may have gone through in the past."[5]

Paramnesia

There are also certain dangers to the operator, such as a charge of unethical conduct. One such danger is what is called paramnesia*. A subject often does not, will not, or cannot differentiate between the sexual fantasies (heterosexual or homosexual) that may occur in hypnosis and the events of everyday life. This kind of danger can be removed by the presence of a third person. Tape recording the process is also helpful.

Symptom Removal

Another danger of hypnosis is in using it for the purpose of "symptom removal" instead of "symptom treatment." We know that pain is a warning sign of physiological disorder and indicates a malfunctioning of the organism. Its removal not only makes diagnosis difficult but may cause a delay in seeking medical treatment. For example, if a person is suffering from a headache and a hypnotist removes the pain by hypnosis, he may jeopardize his life. Such a pain may be the warning sign of a brain tumor (rather than a "nervous tension" headache) and its removal might delay a

---

*Paramnesia is a distortion of mind in which fact and fantasy are confused. With paramnesia, the subject is told under hypnosis that certain types of events have occurred and upon awakening he will remember these fixations as actual facts.

medical diagnosis until the malignancy had grown to a size where it could not be operated on successfully. This is also true with a person who is suffering from a stomach ache. A hypnotist who tries to remove pain may be obscuring a potentially lethal case of appendicitis.

This kind of danger also applies to self-hypnosis. An individual may mistake a particular discomfort or pain for mental anguish when, in reality, it is a warning sign for a serious physiological problem.

The author believes that "symptom removal" should be differentiated from "symptom treatment." "Symptom removal" may be interpreted as the elimination of pain, which is a warning sign of a physical malfunctioning. By removal of this kind of pain the person's life may be put in real danger. "Symptom treatment," on the other hand, is the healing of an ailment by the treatment of the symptom.

With regard to "symptom treatment," there are two schools of thought. The Freudian school, based on psychic determinism, believes that behind a symptom there is a force seeking an outlet—the symptom providing the outlet. If the outlet is blocked by treatment of the symptom, the force will seek another outlet. Accordingly, if a symptom is treated by hypnotic suggestion the "Freudians" claim another symptom will replace it—possibly a worse one. For example, an alcoholic might turn to drugs if his need to drink were to be stopped.

Another school of thought, which seems to be more plausible than the Freudian position, belongs to Conn, Eysenck, Spiegel, LeCron, Kroger, Dorcus, et. al. contend that a very large part of medical treatment is nothing but symptom treatment. They maintain that surgery itself can be symptom treatment. With the removal of a gall bladder, for example, surgery may heal the condition yet the cause of the illness has not been treated. If taking an aspirin results in relief from an ailment, it is not certain that some other ailment will occur in its place.[6]

Furthermore, the sciences of physiology, biology, and neurology have demonstrated that the human mechanism, in contrast to mechanical gadgets, is not a closed system but an open one; you can quiet a heart problem without requiring the patient to break a leg.[7]

Irrespective of what has been explained about the safety of symptom treatment in psychotherapy, it is interesting to consider the following quote from Gibson: [8]

> There is an old saying that when the outer appearance is in good order the inner states will ripen. We say that when we bow our heads and clasp our hands before Buddha, then our reverent feelings well forth. This means that whatever our original feelings may be, they will align themselves with our outer state which we have adjusted. I introduce this into the treatment of neurosis because it takes a long time to build a constructive attitude towards life if we wait for the inner condition to ripen. But we can work more easily from the outer appearance and produce quicker actual results.

Negligence of the Audience

What a hypnotist says in the presence of an audience, but not necessarily to the subject, often has the full power of suggestion. The subject will hear the statements of the hypnotist as proper hypnotic suggestions and will comply with them. For instance, if the hypnotist states that the room is very cold or very warm the subject's senses may respond. Therefore, if the hypnotist deems it necessary to talk to an audience, while an individual subject is experiencing hypnosis, he should first inform the subject that he is about to do so, or give the hypnotized subject a cue or signal (such as touching the shoulder) which means that he is talking to the audience and not to him, etc.

More importantly, the hypnotist should be careful not to permit any member of the audience to ask the subject questions or give him suggestions. Irresponsible individuals may ask the subject questions and cause him embarrassment or interrupt the trance or attempt to give inappropriate suggestions which may cause the subject mental or physical harm.

The hypnotist should always keep in mind that the hypnotized subject is a human being with all his human rights and characteristics, and that he, the hypnotist, is completely responsible for the subject until he has awakened and has left. In this sense, a hypnotized subject's relationship to a hypnotist is similar to the relationship existing between the anesthetized patient and his physician—the patient trusts, and in a sense, is at the mercy of that physician until he has been treated and has left the hospital.

REFERENCES

1. Weitzenhoffer, *General Techniques of Hypnotism*, p. 4.
2. LeCron, *The Complete Guide to Hypnosis* (New York: Harper & Row, Pub., 1971), p. 79.
3. Cheek and LeCron, *Clinical Hypnotherapy*, p. 67.
4. Marcuse, *Hypnosis: Fact and Fiction*, pp. 170-71.
5. Weitzenhoffer, *General Techniques of Hypnotism*, p. 355.
6. Cheek and LeCron, *Clinical Hypnotherapy*, p. 69.
7. Bernhardt and Martin, *Self-Mastery through Self-Hypnosis*, p. 30.
8. Kora, T., "A Method of Instruction in Psychotherapy," Jikeikai Medical Journal (1968), quoted in Gibson, *Hypnosis: Its Nature and Therapeutic Uses*, p. 52.

CHAPTER TWENTY THREE

HOW TO HANDLE RESISTANCE TO HYPNOSIS

Every normal person has the potential to be hypnotized, even develop deep hypnosis; no one is absolutely insusceptible to hypnosis. Therefore the problem of hypnotizing subjects who are resistant to hypnotic induction can be readily managed if the hypnotic procedure conforms to the specific personality of the subject.

The most important causes of adverse reactions to hypnotic induction include fear, tension, uncertainty, "surrender of the will," fear of loss of consciousness, fear of being unable to wake up, fear of revealing personal data—and they all are usually based on misconceptions about hypnosis. For a successful hypnotic induction, the hypnotist has to remove all of these in the pre-induction talk (already discussed in a previous chapter). But if a subject is so terror-stricken about hypnosis that even the hypnotist's persuasive powers fail, then a disguised method of hypnosis should be considered.

There is always a solution to resistance provided the hypnotist does not yield to a negative subject. As Erickson

has stated: "Hypnosis cannot be resisted if there is no hypnosis attempted."[1] An experienced hypnotist not only will
try to remove the resistance of the subject by employing
appropriate techniques, he even utilizes the negative behavior of the subject in favor of the development of hypnosis.
For instance, if an intransigent subject did not agree to be
seated for the hypnotic induction process, the hypnotherapist
might tell him that some people relax more standing than
sitting.

By and large, any attempt to change the subject's behavior,
or force him to comply with things he is not interested in,
works against trance induction. Using appropriate patter
and challenging the ability of the subject is very effective.
For instance, instead of using an authoritarian manner in
the application of the hand levitation technique and commanding the subject to raise his hand, the hypnotist will
use the following patter:

*Now, let us see how the power of your imagination can
affect your muscular activities. Imagine that your body is
so limp and relaxation so deep that your hand is getting
weightless and becoming buoyant. When you focus your
attention on this image, you find that a strange sensation
will prevail in your hand—as if it would like to rise up of
its own accord.*

Sometimes a subject's idiosyncracies can cause resistance.
If the hypnotist tries to correct or alter the attitude of the
subject, the hypnotic induction will fail. In this case, the
hypnotist should try to submit to the subject's idiosyncrasy.
For example, once the writer had a subject who asked if
he could be hypnotized without closing his eyes, since he
did not like to close his eyes. When I realized that he had entered the hypnoidal state and his eyes were getting heavy and

blinking, I suggested to him that he could keep his eyes wide open if he wished, but that it was to his advantage to relax the muscles of the eyes. At this point, the subject closed his eyes voluntarily and developed a deep trance. Had I not complied with his desire, the induction attempt would have failed. Therefore, as a rule, the hypnotist should work with the subject rather than against him.

Sometimes the movement of the subject—scratching some part of the body, laughing, or even smiling during induction indicates resistance.   Other important reasons for resistance of hypnosis are as follows: (1) Extreme tension or anxiety, which deters the subject from focusing his attention sufficiently, (2) Lack of skill and experience on the part of the hypnotist resulting in improper actions, gestures, and suggestions—which are quickly recognized by the subject, (3) Curiosity on the part of the subject (to observe the hypnotic process) with no real intent on being hypnotized, (4) The subject attempts to totally control his own behavior instead of being cooperative and responsive to induction procedure, (5) The subject has an analytical or critical attitude toward the hypnotic process, (6) Over-cooperation on the part of the subject attempting to be hypnotized will work against hypnotic induction (the law of reversed effect), (7) The patter and presentation of ideas by the hypnotist may irritate the subject and make him resistant to hypnotic induction, (8) Being suspicious that the hypnotherapist will make the subject carry out something against his will, (9) Fear that the hypnotherapist will remove addictions such as tranquilizers, pills, etc., and (10) Fear that the hypnotherapist will remove a symptom the subject is not willing to give up (overeating, smoking, etc.).

REFERENCES

1. Erickson and Rossi, *Hypnotherapy: An Exploratory Casebook,* p. 68.

SELF-HYPNOSIS

CHAPTER TWENTY FOUR

SELF-HYPNOSIS

Before you can achieve the kind of life you want, you must become that kind of person. You must think, act, walk, talk, and conduct yourself in all affairs as you wish to become.

Introduction

Self-hypnosis or auto-hypnosis are procedures in which the individual both hypnotizes himself and gives suggestions to himself as effectively as if he were hypnotized by another person. In self-hypnosis the hypnotic state is brought about spontaneously by the individual rather than being induced by another person.

The practice of self-hypnosis is as old as hetero-hypnosis. Indian ascetics, religious people in savage tribes, and faith healers of days gone by, appeared to assume supernatural power and were able to anaesthetize different parts of their bodies spontaneously (enabling them to walk barefooted on a bed of hot coals, or sleep on a bed of nails, etc.) were performing all of those activities through self-hypnosis.

Self-hypnosis entered the scientific armamentarium a hundred years after hetero-hypnosis. The pioneer of self-hypnosis was a young French pharmacist called Emil Coue (1857-1926). For twenty-five years he was practicing hypnotic suggestion using Liebeault's technique and at the same time he was studying the psychology of suggestion. In his studies, Coue observed the influence of waking suggestion in affecting cures, and he came to the conclusion that drugs were often quite ineffective.[1] As one writer pointed out,[2] "Coue has raised the art of self-cure to a truly scientific level." In 1910, Coue established the "neo-Nancy" school and instead of putting his patients under a trance, he depended entirely upon waking suggestion, which he called auto-suggestion. Coue's famous autosuggestion formula is "Every day, in every way, I am getting better and better." In explaining the waking suggestion formula, Coue wrote:

> Therefore every time you have a pain, physical or otherwise, you will go quietly to your room. . . . . sit down and shut your eyes, pass your hand lightly across your forehead if it is mental distress, or upon the part that hurts, if it is pain in any part of the body, and repeat the words: 'It is going, it is going,' etc. very rapidly, ... The essential idea is to say: 'It is going, it is going,' so quickly, that it is impossible for a thought of contrary nature to force itself between the words. We thus actually think it is going, and as all ideas that we fix upon the mind become a reality to us, the pain, physical or mental, vanishes. And should the pain return, repeat the process 10, 20, 50, 100, 200 times if necessary, for it is better to pass the entire day saying: 'It is going!' than to suffer pain and complain about it.[3]

The theories and rules for self-hypnosis are similar to those explained for hetero-hypnosis. There is, however, no direct research to show whether these two phenomena are indeed alike, that is, whether the same abilities, ego functions and personality traits are involved in both.[4]

Hypnosis, whether hetero-hypnosis or self-hypnosis, is not simply an end in itself, but a means that can be used for self-improvement and self-development goals. Self-hypnosis can control physiological pain and improve psychological disorders, and if judiciously used, can be useful for therapeutic purposes. Self-hypnosis and auto-suggestion are methods that can be used to activate mental and physiological forces for our own well being. Through proper utilization of self-hypnosis, many psychogenic and physical disorders can be discovered and corrected. Self-hypnosis can be a valuable aid in eliminating undesirable habits, acquiring constructive habits, creating motivation, changing attitudes, ridding oneself of frustrations, stresses, tensions, and anxieties which are centered in the unconscious mind.[5] By using self-hypnosis we can replace our mentally weak spots with positive thinking, self-affirmation, self confidence, and self-mastery.

Self-hypnosis, through the medium of auto—or self-suggestion, may be used in many areas for the purpose of self-improvement and self-development. It can improve memory, increase the power of concentration, fight procrastination, speed up the ability to learn, stimulate creative ideas and overcome shyness. Moreover, a number of psychosomatic human problems such as insomnia, smoking, alcoholism, drug addiction, nail biting, hair-pulling, torticollis, tinnitus, bed wetting, phobias, undesirable sexual habits and many other psychogenic problems can be controlled by self-hypnosis (unless they are a deep-seated neurotic symptom). Besides these advantages, dental surgery and childbirth can be made painless, and may even feel pleasant, through (self-induced) hypnoanaesthesia—providing sufficient depth is reached.

During World War II, prisoners who were able to hypnotize themselves could better withstand long periods of cold by sending more warm blood to the affected areas.[5]

One of the therapeutic benefits of self-hypnosis is elimination of pain. But, as has already been mentioned, the removal of pain by self-hypnosis should be handled with care. If a pain is organic, a physician should be consulted, but if the pain is psychosomatically oriented, self-hypnosis can be a valuable way to overcome it. Additionally, patients with terminal cancer have been able to spend the last days of their life calmly through the use of self-hypnosis.[6]

Self-hypnosis can play a major role in therapy. Post-hypnotic suggestion that a doctor gives to a patient may last a few days, a few hours, or a few minutes. However long they last, post-hypnotic suggestion, usually wears off and will rarely be sufficient for the patient until his next visit to the doctor.

Since the doctor only sees the patient once or twice weekly, the patient has to renew the influence of post-hypnotic suggestion himself by doing self-hypnosis several times a day. By doing so he makes the therapeutic suggestion continuous from one session to the next. The ability to help oneself in therapy through auto-suggestion, under the supervision of a doctor, has two advantages. First, self-hypnosis could work better than any drugs a doctor might prescribe. Second, the patient begins to rely on himself for his treatment rather than being completely dependant upon his doctor. As a rule, the person who practices self-hypnosis is placing his faith not on an outside entity but on his own mind.

As with heter-hypnosis, in self-hypnosis a deep hypnotic relaxation is not necessary for therapeutic purposes. A person can produce only a light degree of self-hypnosis and give therapeutic suggestions to himself. Usually a depth score of 13 on the Davis-Husband scale and a depth score of 20 to 24 on the LeCron-Bordeaux scale is ideal for self-hypnosis.

Self-hypnosis has many other advantages. For example, during working hours when a person is feeling tired, or he is inefficient at work, a short self-induction with proper suggestions will make one feel vigorous, energetic, and refreshed in body, mind, and spirit.

Despite the fact that many writers have asserted that self-hypnosis is easy to achieve, in my opinion, self induction is not that simple. This is particularly true with deeper degrees of self-hypnosis. Therefore, when hetero-hypnosis is compared with self-hypnosis, experience shows that the former is far easier to achieve than the latter. The reason probably lies in the fact that the subject has a dual function in self-hypnosis. He has to be passive to be hypnotized and at the same time he must take an active role in the induction of hypnotic trance.

In hetero-hypnosis, Fromm states that the subject's ego, while listening to the hypnotist's patter, is divided into an experiencing part and an observing part (the "Listener," and "Observer"). But in self-hypnosis, where the subject gives the suggestions to himself, the ego is split into three parts: The "Speaker," "Listener," and "Observer"[7]

Whereas induction of self-hypnosis is far more difficult than hetero-hypnosis, learning and teaching self-hypnosis, on the other hand, is much easier than hetero-hypnosis. In effect, self-hypnosis can be taught by physicians to their patients in only 20 or 30 minutes. Complete mastery of self-hypnosis is achieved through conscientious practice.

To learn self-hypnosis, as with any other skill, one has to

practice patiently, Kroger, a leading authority in medical hypnosis states, "Do not expect immediate results when you begin to use auto-hypnosis, and don't ask, 'What's wrong?' . . . . . Don't think that you have to be 'out of this world' to be in auto-hypnosis. . . . . You may develop a feeling of detachment. You may experience a very pleasant sinking feeling, or you may get a feeling of peace and serenity. At times you may not even feel a definite change: it may just seem as if you had your eyes closed and heard everything at all times. However, if you aim for a deeply relaxed state, you will reach it.[8]

Preparation for Self-Hypnosis

Some popular techniques of self-hypnosis are explained in the next section. Regardless of which technique a person chooses for self-hypnosis, the physical and mental conditions listed below should be met before and during the induction of self-hypnosis.

(1) Quiet. The person must choose a quiet place for self-hypnosis. His clothing should be loose and comfortable. He should sit in a comfortable easy chair or lie down on a comfortable couch or bed. If sitting on a chair, the hands should rest on the lap and the feet flat on the floor with the legs extended. If using a couch or bed, the person should lie down flat on his back. The legs should be uncrossed and the feet about eight inches apart so that the thighs do not touch. The arms should be parallel to the body, fingers loosely outstretched, and palms downward. A flat pillow may be used.

For the best results, self-hypnosis should be done in the

same place, at the same time, and even in the same chair or couch, every time. The reason is that environmental conditions and time are a part of the "mental set" that condition the person to self-hypnosis.

(2) Environmental Conditions. All the environmental conditions explained for hetero-hypnosis including temperature, light, odors, dress and physical condition of the subject should be met for self-hypnosis as well.

(3) Breathing. The person should take a few deep breaths, the last one being a hyperventilation.*

(4) Concentration. The person should have the ability to concentrate his attention and to make his mind blank.

(5) Faith. The person should consciously and unconsciously have faith in hypnosis. If an individual approaches self-hypnosis with a "prove it to me" attitude, he will not produce it.

(6) Motivation. The person must have sufficient motivation to undergo self-hypnosis. Mere curiosity or amusement can not be considered relevant motivation for self-hypnosis. In hetero-hypnosis an experienced hypnotist can circumvent the weak motivation of the subject and hypnotize him, but in self-hypnosis, as the subject is alone, sufficient motivation is necessary for the subject to go under trance.

---

*Hyperventilation is a long, deep inhaling, holding the breath for about 5 seconds and then immediate exhaling (inhaling through the nose, and exhaling through the mouth). Weitzenhoffer[9] believed that hyperventilation raises the individual's suggestibility. Sargant and Frazer believed that hyperventilation alone could induce hypnosis provided that the person concentrates on his breathing. [10]

(7) Imagination. Imagination can be considered the fuel of the mind machinery which brings about hypnosis. It is so important to hypnotic induction that even negative aspects of the mind, like fear and anger, can be utilized as stimuli for producing hypnosis. When the subject accepts departure from reality through imagination, hypnosis is assured. Therefore, the subject must know how to use his imagination in order to achieve self-hypnosis. That is why, as has already been mentioned, imaginative people are good hypnotic subjects.

(8) Mental Set. During the preparation for self-hypnosis, and also throughout the induction period, the person has to repeat in his mind over and over the statement, "positive thinking brings me the advantages that I desire." Let us call this image symbol "55." Reviewing this image in the mind helps the person to rid his mind of intrusive thoughts, eliminates distraction, and focus attention on self-hypnotic relaxation—thus facilitating the advent of hypnosis. In brief, this image enables the person to gain what is termed "mental set," that is, being conditioned to relax physically as well as mentally for the purpose of achieving self-hypnosis.

(9) Use of the "Key Word" in the Hypnoidal State. Before we discuss the "key word" in the hypnoidal state, we should understand the phenomenon involved. The hypnoidal state in hypnosis is quite similar to hypnogogic in natural sleep. Hypnogogic is a pre-sleep state which is associated with drowsiness, reverie, and haze. It is a transitional condition between the waking state and natural sleep. Although the person in this state is still conscious, his critical thinking is depressed. He is detached from his environment and his attention fluctuates more toward abstraction. The

hypnoidal state in hypnosis similar to the hypnogogic state in natural sleep. This term refers to a condition which is neither waking nor hypnosis but lies between the two. The hypnoidal state is a twilight state characterized by complete physical and mental relaxation, drowsiness, fluttering and closing of the eyelids. (During the hypnoidal state "thinking" seems to become "sensing."). When this state emerges, a feeling of heaviness envelops the person, consciousness fluctuates—and, on the whole, the suggestibility of the person increases. [11] The "key word" is a pre-suggestion phrase that the person should choose for self-conditioning. The significance of the "key word" should, of course, be its meaning to the subject. It should be something such as *relax, relax now, meditate,* etc. During the induction of self-hypnosis, when the person feels the emergence of the hypnoidal state, rapid recitation of the "key word" should then take place. Through conditioning, that is, using the same "key word" at this same point (attainment of the hypnoidal state) and every single time self-hypnosis is attempted, the "key word" eventually means self-hypnosis to the subject. The hypnoidal state becomes the hypnotic state instantly and automatically—but not without the necessary conditioning and practice.

Techniques of Self-Hypnosis

As with hetero-hypnosis there is almost no limit to the variety of techniques for inducing self-hypnosis. And, again, as with hetero-hypnosis, no technique should be considered superior to another. Some methods may meet a given individual's needs better than others. Naturally, with experience, each individual will develop his own favorite method and condition himself with it.

When a person becomes conditioned to hypnosis, he will be able to hypnotize himself in a matter of seconds. The most important point for production of self-hypnosis is to relax and let it happen. If a person tries too hard, he will become tense which interferes with his relaxation. If he has a negative attitude, he will also hinder the production of self-hypnosis. But if the person has a sincere and unreserved desire to enter the state of hypnosis, then he can achieve it properly.

Linder states three fundamental attitudes which should accompany the induction of self-hypnosis:

(1) 'I want this to happen.' Remember hypnosis is a consent state of mind.

(2) 'I expect this to happen.' Generate a belief in your ability to achieve what millions before you have attained. Remember hypnosis is just another one of nature's normal states.

(3) 'I will watch it happen.' Once you begin to respond properly do not hinder the carrying out of suggestion by letting your critical factor re-enter and change your mood.[12]

There are a number of mechanical aids that can help a person to induce self-hypnosis and deepen the hypnotic trance. These mechanical aids include hypnotic crystal balls, metronomes, hand hypnodiscs, hypnodisc spirals, and an oscillating hand that moves back and forth with a gentle audible sound. Some of these aids may suit the individual needs of a person, some may not. If a person wants to take advantage of one of these mechanical aids, he has to choose it on the basis of his psychological preference. A spiral disc, a useful aid for both self-hypnosis and hetero-hypnosis, is placed on a phonograph player and as it revolves, the person concentrates his eyes on the whirling center of the disc and induces self-hypnosis. Concentrating on the revolving spiral helps put the person in the proper frame of mind for hypnosis.

One of the easisest ways to induce self-hypnosis is to record your own hypnotic induction or have someone else with a good speaking voice read it to you. The patter should be properly worded, soothing, and monotonal. Deepening procedures can also be carried out by listening to a tape made for this purpose.

To be most effective, these tapes should be recorded in the second person, i.e. instead of saying: "My body is getting numb and heavy," you should say: "Your body is getting numb and heavy." This is because in the induction process your conscious mind is the hypnotist and your unconscious mind, the subject.

Some of the most popular techniques of self-hypnotic induction are as follows:

Progressive Relaxation Technique

Seat yourself in a comfortable chair with your feet flat on the floor, your hands resting on your lap while leaning back on the chair. Then you should meet the conditions explained in the previous discussion (preparation for self-hypnosis), including fixing your eyes on a spot on the wall above your eye level or on the ceiling.

After about 15 seconds of gazing at the chosen spot, close your eyes and raise one of your feet and hold it horizontally at the height of your hip. Then curl your toes and squeeze them as hard as you can. Relax your toes; let them be limp and loose; and while doing this, focus your thoughts on the symbol "55." (Remember, the symbol "55" signifies the statement "Positive thinking brings me the advantages I desire." You should condition yourself so that whenever you think of the number "55," this statement will appear in your mind). Next, bend your ankle upward so that your foot points up toward your body. Then let it relax as you think of symbol "55." Now, stiffen the muscles of your leg from the toes right up to the hip. Tighten the calf muscles and those in the thigh as much as you can until it is a little bit painful. Then let your foot drop heavily to the floor and relax while thinking over and over of symbol "55." Repeat exactly the same procedure with your other leg.

Next, raise one of your arms and hold it in a horizontal position. Then bend your wrist up and push it straight toward the ceiling with your fingers extended. Next, slowly curl your fingers into a clenched fist. Tense your arm muscles from the finger tips up to the shoulder and neck, until you feel discomfort and pain in them. Then let your arm drop heavily on your lap, thinking again of symbol "55." Apply the same procedure to your other arm.

Now, exercise your abdominal muscles. Make them as rigid and stiff as possible and hold them that way for a few seconds until you feel the strain. Then, relax them, thinking of symbol "55."

Now, concentrate on your chest muscles. Tighten your chest muscles as much as possible, and hold them for a few seconds until you feel the strain. Then let them relax while you think of symbol "55."

Having completed the previous exercise, hold your neck stiff and tense the neck muscles. Next, slowly move your head from side to side several times, keeping tension in all the muscles of your neck for a few seconds. Then make your neck muscles relax and review the symbol "55" in your mind's eye. Now, turn your attention to your facial muscles. Squeeze your eyes tightly shut, move your jaws from side to side and press your lips together. These movements make your facial muscles tighten. Then let them go limp and think of symbol "55."

When all these procedures have been completed, remain motionless for a few moments, enjoying the relaxation of every muscle in your body. These procedures will eliminate distraction and facilitate the advent of your hypnoidal state. Upon feeling the emergence of the hypnoidal state, you then mention your "key word" mentally or verbally and thus enter into hypnotic relaxation. When you achieve the hypnotic state, you may wish to deepen your trance by employing the deepening procedures explained in the next discussion.

Whether you wish to deepen your trance or not, this is the precise time to give yourself relevant, positive suggestion the exact nature of which will be explained later.

Relaxation Technique

Sit in a comfortable chair or lie down on a couch or bed. Meet the preparatory procedures. Then with your eyes closed, focus your attention on your toes. Imagine that a warm, soothing sensation is entering the toes of one of your feet. During the entire procedure, think occasionally of the image "55." Then feel a warm, restful sensation gradually spreading over the rest of your feet. Next, feel this pleasant sensation creeping up toward your ankle. . . . . still further up throughout your leg. . . . . into your knee and your thigh . . . . . you now feel this warm peaceful sensation gradually spreading over the rest of your feet. Next, feel this pleasant sensation creeping up toward your ankle . . . . still further up and throughout your leg into your knee and thigh . . . You now feel this warm and peaceful sensation gradually entering your pelvic area . . . . Next, try to imagine and feel the same sensation in your other toes . . . into your ankle, your leg, your knee, your thigh, and into your pelvic area. You associate this pleasant restful sensation with the image "55." Then feel this warm pleasant sensation running upward toward your abdominal muscles . . . . Next, feel it creeping up toward your chest muscles, and from there into your shoulder muscles, flowing down through your arms and your hands into your fingertips . . . . Now feel this wonderful sensation traveling back through your hands, your arms, your shoulders and into the muscles of your neck, and from there into your facial muscles . . . . . Now, pause a few moments and feel this warm pleasant sensation in the muscles of all parts of your face . . . . in the muscles near your eyes, in your cheeks, jaw, and lips . . . . Think of "55." . . . . Then feel this warm, soothing sensation creeping up through your neck into your head, and from there into your spinal cord . . . . All parts of your body, from your toes right up to the very top of your scalp are electrified by a pleasant soothing sensation. Every muscle, every fiber, every tissue in your body is relaxed.

Having completed this procedure, you should enter the hypnoidal state. As soon as you feel the emergence of the hypnoidal state mention your "key word" and slip into hypnosis. Then deepen your trance, and give yourself proper auto-suggestions.

Subjective Technique

Sit in a comfortable chair or lie down on a couch or bed; fix your eyes on a spot on the wall above eye level or on the ceiling. Try to meet all the preparatory requirements for self-hypnosis. Then focus your attention on your eyelids. During the procedure occasionally think of the symbol "55."

Now, first imagine that your eyelids are becoming very heavy. Try to feel this heaviness. Again and again tell yourself mentally: 'My eyes are getting very heavy. I feel my eyes getting very heavy, and the heavier they become, the more comfortable and relaxed I feel. It seems that it is becoming impossible for me to keep my eyelids open. It really feels so good to close my eyes. I am going to count to three. When I complete the count, it will be absolutely impossible for me to keep my eyes open. ONE ... my eyes are narrowing to a slit. They are about to close. TWO ... my eyelids are going to drop involuntarily. THREE ... they are closing ... they are closing ... they are closing.'

(Then tell yourself) 'My eyelids are now locked together, they are stuck fast, so tightly stuck that I cannot open them. Now, do not try any longer ... I can open my eyes whenever I choose but will keep them closed for the remainder of the induction.'

Now think of a peaceful scene. Imagine you are walking around a swimming pool in the middle of a beautiful garden. It is mid-spring. The weather is very pleasant. It is 3 o'clock in the afternoon. You keep walking along side the pool. All around the pool are red, white, and yellow roses. Alongside the pool are jasmin trees. A mild breeze blows from the flowers, bringing you the sweet smell of roses and jasmin.

As you continue walking, the sweet jasmin scent stays with you. Suddenly, a few yards from the pool, you see a hammock stretched between two shady trees. You decide to lie down in that hammock in the midst of the beautiful garden and enjoy a deep relaxation. So, you approach the hammock, you lie down in it, and find it very comfortable and relaxing. You feel so relaxed and comfortable that ten minutes of actual time pass like one minute. As you enjoy your relaxed state, a pretty bird lands on the branch of a tree in front of you. You keep looking at it. After a few seconds the bird leaves its perch and starts to fly toward you. It is getting closer and closer to you. You wish to follow the movements of the bird, but the beauty of the scene causes you to close your eyes and go under a very deep sleep.

This imagery may work as a very pleasant method of induction and take you into a deep hypnotic trance. Any variation of this scene which suits individual needs can be applied for the induction of self-hypnosis. You may even tape a scene like the above, and listen to it.

Obviously, in the entire induction process, every now and then, you have to think of the symbol "55." At the the time of the emergence of the hypnoidal state you should use your "key word" and switch yourself into self-hypnosis.

Combination Method

Seat yourself in a comfortable chair with your feet flat on the floor, your legs extended, and your hands on your thighs or on the arms of the chair. Meet the preparatory rules for self-hypnosis. Fix your gaze on something.

Begin counting slowly from 1 to 10. Say the number ONE, direct your attention on your eyes and tell yourself

repeatedly, 'my eyes are getting heavy, very heavy. I feel
my eyes becoming so heavy that at the count of 3 I will
not be able to keep them open—they will close automatically.' Count to 2 and think of the symbol "55." Roll your
eyes up into the back of your head, then count to three
and tell yourself, 'My eyelids are so heavy now that I cannot
open them. It is just as if they were glued together . . . .
I now go deeper into self-relaxation, I am able to open
my eyes whenever I choose, but will keep them closed
for the remainder of the induction.'

Next, count to 4, think of the symbol "55," and
give yourself the following suggestions: 'My toes, feet,
calves, and legs are getting very heavy. I feel a tingling sensation all over my legs. It feels very nice. Both my legs,
from my toes up to the pelvic area, feel so relaxed, heavy,
and limp. So relaxed that they almost feel stuck to the
floor . . .I now go deeper into self-relaxation, I am able
to move my legs whenever I choose, and I now go even
deeper into self-relaxation.'

Now, count to 5, think of the symbol "55," and say
to yourself: 'I feel my abdominal muscles becoming numb
and heavy. Even the pit of my stomach is becoming wooden-
like and relaxed.'

Count to 6, think of the image "55," and continue telling yourself: 'Now I can feel the muscles in my chest becoming relaxed. I am breathing more regularly and more
easily . . . . (Then thinking, now and then, of the symbol
"55," continue counting and with the count of 7, tell yourself): 'Now I feel a numb, wooden-like sensation in my fingers, wrists, hands, arms, and forearms. My arms feel just
as though I have been sleeping on them. EIGHT—the muscles of my neck, my entire body, from my neck down, are

relaxed. NINE—I feel my facial muscles becoming loose. My head is also very light. TEN—Now I feel that my spinal cord is very heavy and at the same time very relaxed and refreshed . . . . my whole body feels loose and limp, from the top of my head right down to my toes . . . . with every breath that I take, I can feel myself drifting into a deeper and deeper relaxation.'

Then you have to visualize a relaxed and pleasant scene like the one described in the "subjective technique." This can be some pleasant scene in your past, or a scene you imagine in the future. It can be a peaceful, mountainous scene, a blue sky with one or two billowy clouds moving slowly. On a lake with a sailboat floating gently, or any scene that makes you feel good, drowsy, and relaxed will do.

The "key word" and suggestions should be given at the appropriate times.

Spiegel's Technique

To teach their patients how to hypnotize themselves and reinforce their therapeutic suggestions psychiatrists Herbert and David Spiegel describe an interesting method in their current book:

You sit or lie down, and to yourself, you count to three. At one, you do one thing; at two, you do two things; and at three you do three things. In all you carry out six things. At one, look up toward your eyebrows; at two, while looking up, close your eyelids and take a deep breath; and, at three exhale, let your eyes relax, and let your body float.

As you feel yourself floating, you permit one hand or the other to feel like a buoyant balloon and let it float upward. When it reaches this upright position, it becomes the signal for you to enter a state of meditation.

This floating sensation signals your mind to turn inward and pay attention to your own thoughts—like private meditation. Ballet dancers and athletes float all the time. That is why they concentrate and coordinate their movements so well. When they do not float they are tense and do not do as well. 13

Then the Spiegels advise their patients that in the beginning they should do these exercises as often as ten different times a day, preferably every one or two hours. At first the exercise takes a minute, but as the patient becomes more expert, he can do it much less time.

According to the Spiegels, the patient, to de-hypnotize himself, should count backwards in this manner:

Now, three, get ready. Two, with your eyelids closed, roll up your eyes. And One, let your eyelids open slowly. Then when your eyes are back in focus, slowly make a fist with the hand that is up, and as you open your fist slowly, your usual sensation and control returns. Let your hand float downward. 14

Post-hypnotic Suggestion Technique

The best way to learn self-hypnosis is to have a professional hypnotist give you a post-hypnotic suggestion so that in the future you are able to achieve self-hypnosis. The operator will hypnotize you rather deeply and convince your unconscious mind that every time you wish to hypnotize yourself, by performing a certain procedure—such as counting forwards or backwards, and mentioning a key word or a signal, you will automatically go into hypnosis. This hetero-hypnotic suggestion must be reinforced several times daily by re-suggesting the same thing to yourself while in self-hypnosis until you master the technique. This acts as the stimulus for the conditioned response which promotes self-hypnosis.

You can also give yourself a post-hypnotic suggestion—with the result that at each succeeding session of self-hypnosis, you will go quickly into a deeper and sounder self-hypnotic relaxation.

Deepening Procedures of Self-Hypnosis

Although light or deep trance have the same effect for the unconscious mind to assimilate the auto-suggestion, to deepen auto-hypnosis, a number of techniques can be applied, some of which are common to hetero-hypnosis.

Visual Imagery Technique—This is one of the best techniques for deepening self-hypnosis. You imagine yourself in any situation that gives you peace and serenity. For instance, you may see yourself lying down comfortably in your bed, enjoying a sound sleep and pleasant dreams; or you may be lying in a hammock, or lying on a beach and watching the ocean waves, or any similarly relaxing imagery. As you imagine yourself in such desirable conditions, concentrate on drifting deeper and deeper into relaxation.

Escalator Technique—You may imagine yourself riding down an elevator or an escalator. Then you start counting slowly to yourself from 20 down to 0. You should think to yourself that the further the escalator goes down, the deeper you go into hypnosis. Also, between each number you may imagine yourself drifting deeper into relaxation.

Counting Method—You may count from 100 forward or backward, and by one's, two's, three's, four's, etc. With every count you should imagine yourself going deeper into hypnosis.

Deepening self-hypnosis requires the same kind of practice or conditioning as the induction of hypnosis. Therefore, with every count, you should coordinate your bodily functioning (ideomotor) with your thoughts (ideosensory). For instance, you should designate a particular number by which time you feel your mind is separated from your body, etc.

Hand Levitation Method—You may suggest hand levitation to yourself and imagine that when your fingers touch your face, your arm will immediately become heavy and fall to your thigh. As this happens, you go deeper into hypnosis than ever before.

Post-hypnotic Suggestion—As with hetero-hypnosis, each time you hypnotize yourself you can give the suggestion that the next time you attempt self-hypnosis you will go more quickly and more deeply into the hypnotic state.

Deepening self-hypnosis can be assisted by means of a tape recording made specifically for that purpose. Using a tape is preferred by some people because they feel that less of a conscious effort is required by the subject during deepening procedures.

Tests of Self-Hypnosis

To recongnize whether you are self-hypnotized, and if so to what depth, you may give yourself a number of tests. It is best not to attempt giving any test to yourself or attempt to produce any hypnotic phenomena until you have practiced self-hypnosis successfully several times. However, when you are sure of achieving the state of self-hypnosis, then you can give relevant tests to yourself. If you respond properly to the tests, then you know you are self-hypnotized.

Tests of self-hypnosis are very similar to the hetero-hypnotic depth tests mentioned in a previous chapter. The only difference between self-hypnosis tests and hetero-hypnosis depth tests is that in the latter the hypnotist gives you the tests but in the former the tests are self-managed.

Eye Catalepsy Test—After having achieved relaxation and eye closure, suggest to yourself that your eyelids are getting very heavy and that they are locked together. You may word your suggestion like this: "ONE, my eyelids are locked together. TWO, my eyelids are actually so glued together that it will be an enormous task to move them. THREE, they are stuck fast, tight, very tight." As you mention the word "tight"—preferably mentally—try to open them, but stop trying as soon as you are unable to do so. When you respond in a satisfactory manner to the test suggestion, give yourself the following suggestion and continue on with induction procedure: "Now my eyes are perfectly normal in every way, and I can open them whenever I choose, but will keep them closed for the remainder of the induction. I am now going even deeper into self-hypnosis." If you respond properly to this test then you can be sure that you are hypnotized.

Arm Catalepsy Test—Levitate one of your hands and suggest to yourself that it is getting rigid and taut, and you cannot bring it down again. After you respond successfully to this test, suggest to yourself that your arm has become loose and limp and is going to drop on your thigh. Include in your suggestion the idea that when your hand touches your thigh you will go to an even deeper stage of hypnosis.

Another variation of this test is that you suggest to yourself that your hand is getting very heavy, that it is stuck to the arm of the chair, and that you cannot move it or lift it up.

Hand Levitation Test—Imagine that one of your hands is beginning to lose all sensation of weight, and is becoming buoyant. At the count of three, your rising fingers will touch your face. (Suggest to yourself that this will be done involuntarily and without conscious effort). After your fingers have touched your face, let your arm drop on your lap and imagine that upon dropping your hand on your thigh, you will develop a much deeper state of hypnosis.

Foot Test—This test can be accomplished while sitting or lying down. First you imagine that one of your feet is very heavy. You imagine that your foot is so heavy that it is stuck to the floor and you are not able to move it or raise it. The harder you try to raise your foot, the less you will be able to do it—until you reach a certain count.

Glove Anaesthesia Test—You can give glove anaesthesia suggestions to yourself and test the success of your hypnotic trance by responding positively to it. To produce glove anaesthesia you should rub the back of one of your hands clockwise or counterclockwise, and suggest to yourself that by rubbing your hand it becomes numb, senseless, and wooden-like. You will lose all sensation in that hand and you will feel no pain if the hand is stimulated.

You may also suggest to yourself that glove anaesthesia will develop in your hand simultaneously with hand levitation, and will remain in your hand until a certain period of time after awakening. Wording of the suggestion should be something like this: "Upon awakening, my left (or right) hand will be numb, cold, and senseless for one minute." When anaesthesia is affected in your hand, you will feel a little pressure on the spot that you choose to pinch, but no pain.

If you succeed in passing these tests, you can be sure that you have developed a medium stage of hypnosis. As you keep practicing, a greater depth of hypnosis will be produced.

Auto-Suggestion

After you are satisfied that you have achieved self-hypnosis, you can make suggestions to yourself (auto-suggestion). Suggestion is actually the sole agent of hypnosis and the exclusive means of behavior modification. When a person suggests thoughts or ideas to himself, he has already reasoned them out and has faith in them. We know that all forms of hypnosis are, in fact, self-hypnosis. Hypnosis occurs "inside" the hypnotized individual, and it is not an external event.[15] Even in hetero-hypnosis the suggestions of the hypnotist do not take effect without the unconscious agreement of the subject. We know that whenever there is a clash between the conscious and unconscious minds, it is the unconscious mind that will win out. Therefore, for a suggestion to be carried out by the conscious mind, acceptance by the unconscious mind is necessary.

It follows that auto-suggestion is usually much more

meaningful than suggestion administered by someone else. Moreover, when a person gives suggestion to himself he will, in fact, participate directly and more actively in his behavior modification goals than when induced to do so by another person.

A very important part of auto-suggestion is the relationship between the conscious and the unconscious mind, and their way of communicating with each other. Where hetero-hypnosis is concerned no problem will arise; the hypnotist tries to bypass the conscious mind of the subject and attempts to implant the suggestion in the subject's unconscious. But in self-hypnosis the situation is not so simple; difficulty arises because the hypnotic state cannot develop unless conscious activities recede. Yet, the conscious mind has the power to formulate suggestion. Therefore, the question arises as to what part of the mind implements the suggestion.

The authors of various books on self-hypnosis talk about four kinds of auto-suggestion: verbal, mental, pictorial, and pre-hypnotic. Verbal auto-suggestion is given by the subject—either aloud or by whispering. Mental auto-suggestion is reviewed in the mind in the manner of thinking. Pictorial auto-suggestion is a visual image that the person "sees" in his mind. Pre-hypnotic suggestion, developed by Arons,[16] is when suggestion is given before hypnotizing oneself.

The author believes that the most effective method of auto-suggestion is probably a combination of pre-hypnotic and pictorial suggestions. The person will word his suggestion after meeting the preparatory conditions, and before self-hypnosis. When he has achieved self-hypnosis, his visual image will reflect his suggestion.

There seems to be certain advantages to this method. For one thing, the suggestions that the person has already recited will linger in his unconscious mind, and without any conscious effort, continue to remain in his mind. The person need not do anything consciously. The recited suggestions automatically will be retained and nurtured in the unconscious, and will hold exclusive sway over his thinking. This mental mechanism will be fully automatic, effortless, and will reside in the unconscious mind. This method of auto-suggestion actually eliminates the previously discussed problem of the receding of the conscious mind and its inability to communicate auto-suggestion to the unconscious mind.

In conveying suggestions to the unconscious mind, picture images seem to be more effective than words. This is because the unconscious mind understands pictures better than words. A picture is, indeed, worth a thousand words as Confucius stated many centuries ago. For instance, if a person is supposed to give himself a suggestion to overcome stage fright, it is not enough to suggest to himself: "In public speaking, I feel completely self-confident." Rather, these words should be reinforced with a mental picture of the person as a successful speaker, speaking before a large audience—smiling, self-assured, and feeling exhilarated. The person must "see" the image of himself as the successful person he wants to be.

Rules of Auto-Suggestion

For auto-suggestions to be more effective, a number of rules should be followed:

(1) Suggestions should be condensed, revised, and perfected on a piece of paper or a small card and read several times prior to the induction of self-hypnosis.

(2) Auto-suggestion should be direct, permissive, and positive. Negative words and phrases such as "not," "can't," "won't," etc. should be avoided. For instance, instead of suggesting (for a simple nervous tension headache), "Upon awakening, my headache will be gone," it would be better to suggest, "My head is feeling clear and better; I am becoming more and more comfortable and tranquil in every way." Or instead of saying, "When I sit for my job interview, I will not feel nervous and tense," it is better to say, "When I sit for my job interview, I feel calm, serene, and creative."

Another advantage of applying this procedure is that the unconscious mind will be given sufficient time to assimilate the idea.

(3) The suggestion should be combined with a motive that enhances the effectiveness of the suggestion. This may be done through visual imagery. For instance, when a person gives himself a suggestion to overcome tension at the time of a job interview, he may envision getting a good, prestigious position.

(4) Suggestions should be given singularly. The unconscious mind cannot deal with more than one idea at a time. Additionally, the suggestion should be repeated and reinforced in successive hypnotic sessions until the desired goal is achieved.

(5) Auto-suggestions should be positively and logically worded and capable of being fulfilled.

Waking from Self-Hypnosis

To awaken from self-hypnosis (or more properly termed, to return to one's normal state of awareness) all you have to do is to suggest that you are going to do just that. This can be done in several ways:

(1) Suggest to yourself that on the count of three you will be wide awake, refreshed, relaxed, and full of energy.

(2) Envision the face of a clock set at the time you wish to awaken.

(3) Think about the length of time you wish to remain under a trance (this should be done prior to self-hypnosis), and the specific time you wish to wake up.

When you first start practicing self-hypnosis, you may drop off into a natural sleep. To avoid this, you can suggest to yourself that you will count back from 20 to 0, and at the count of 20 you will be under a trance. Once you have achieved the hypnotic state, and after you have accomplished auto-suggestion, you count from 1 to 5, and at the count of 5, you wake up.

When you are about to wake up, always suggest to yourself that upon waking, you will feel relaxed, refreshed, clear-headed, full of energy, and happy.

REFERENCES

1. Hull, *Hypnosis and Suggestibility,* p. 17.
2. Duckworth, J., *How to Use Auto-Suggestion Effectively* (Hollywood, CA.: Wilshire Book Co., 1960), p. 82.
3. Emile Coue, *How to Practice Suggestion and Auto-Suggestion* (New York: American Library Service, 1923), pp. 81-82.
4. Fromm, E., "Quo Vadis Hypnosis? Predictions of Future Trends in Hypnosis Research," in *Hypnosis: Research Developments and Perspectives,* ed. E. Fromm and R. Shor (New York: Aldine Atherton, 1972), p. 579.
5. Marcuse, *Hypnosis: Fact and Fiction,* p. 201.
6. Cheek and LeCron, *Clinical Hypnotherapy,* p. 64.

7.   Fromm, E., *Hypnosis: Research Developments and Perspectives,* p. 579.
8.   Kroger, *Clinical and Experimental Hypnosis,* pp. 78-88.
9.   Weitzenhoffer, *General Techniques of Hypnotism,* pp. 157&297.
10. Sargant and Frazer, "Inducing Light Hypnosis by Hyperventilation," *Lancet,* 235: 778-79, 1938.
11. Weitzenhoffer, *General Techniques of Hypnotism,* p. 48.
12. Lindner, P., *Mind Over Platter* (Hollywood, CA.: Wilshire Book Co., 1963), p. 78.
13. Spiegel, *Trance and Treatment,* pp. 211-12.
14. *Ibid.*
15. Cooke and Van Vogt, *The Hypnotism Handbook,* p. 48.
16. Arons, H., *Handbook of Self-Hypnosis* (S. Orange, NJ: Power Publishers, 1964), pp. 69-70.

NAME INDEX

A

Arons, H., VIII, 32, 35, 53, 56,
78, 82, 94, 104, 106,
112-114, 120, 122, 217,
221
Arons' Scale, 119, 149, 168

B

Barber, T. X., VIII, 24, 27,
178, 180
Bass, M., 21
Bernhard, R., 18, 21, 35, 41,
186
Bernheim, H., 9, 10, 12, 17,
23, 86, 88, 92
Bertrand, A., 8
Bjornstorm, F., 56
Bordeaux, J., 48, 122
Braid, J., 7-9, 15, 86, 88
Brenman, M., 25, 27
Breur, J., 12
Brown, M., 27
Brunett, C. T., 165, 179
Buddha, 185

C

Charcot, J. M., 10-12, 17, 22,
86, 101
Cheek, D., 90, 92, 161, 180,
186, 220
Confucius, 218
Conn, J. H., 142, 146, 184
Cooke, C. E., VIII, 25, 28,
221
Cooper, L., 38, 128, 137, 164,
179
Coue, E., 23, 143, 144, 194 ,
220

D

Dahl, Dr., 38
Dauven, J., 104
Dean, J., VII
de Faria, J. C., 5, 8, 88
de Jussieu, A. L., 3
Deleuze, J. P. F., 5
de Milechnin, 120, 122
de Puysegur, M., 4, 5
Donanto, 10
Dorcus, R. M., 23, 27, 155,
157, 184
Duckworth, J., 220

E

Edwards, G., 151
Einstein, A., 38
Ellen, A., VII
Elliotson, J., 5, 6
Erickson, Elizabeth M., 148,
150, 151
Erickson; Milton, VIII, 13, 19-21,
23, 38, 69, 81, 82, 101,
105, 107, 110-114, 122,
130, 131, 137, 146, 148,
150, 151, 163, 164, 166,
167, 169, 179, 181, 187,
190
Esdaile, J., 6, 84
Estabrooks, G. H., 27, 179
Eysenck, H. J., 184

F

Farber, 177
Faw, V., 34, 35
Feldman, S., 180
Fezler, W., 14, 28
Fisher, 178, 180
Franklin, B., 3
Frazer, 199, 221
Freud, S., 9, 11-14, 25, 27,
42-44, 50, 172, 184

223

SUBJECT INDEX

A

abreaction, 13, 178
age regression, 112, 119, 129,
166-172, 174, 178, 182,
183
acrophobia, 108
alcoholism, 193
alpha activity, 16
amnesia, 120, 127-129, 132,
147-149, 165, 171, 172,
175, 185
  complete, 116, 120, 127
149, 160
  partial, 116, 118, 127, 149
  post-hypnotic, 128, 129
  selective, 120
  spontaneous, 128
  suggestive, 128
  systematic post-hypnotic,
118
  total, 20, 165
anaesthesia, 127, 129-132, 176,
176, 182, 213, 214
  chemo, 6, 130
  complete, 118
  hypno, 131, 133
  partial, 120
analgesia, 120, 129
anti-social acts, 19, 20
arm rising and falling test, 60
auto-hypnosis, 191, 193, 196,
210
automatic writing, 174, 175
auto-suggestion, 192, 194, 204,
210, 214, 215-218
  direct, 217
  mental, 215
  permissive, 217
  pictorial, 215
  positive, 217
  rules of, 216
  verbal, 215

B

Babinski reflex, 167
backward postural sway test, 64
bed wetting, 193
behavior modification, 46, 215
Bible, 51
blood circulation, 17
British Medical Association, 6, 14
British Society of Medical Hyp-
nosis, 36
British Society of Medical Hyp-
notists, VII

C

catalepsy,
  arm, 112, 125
  complete, 118
  eye, 112, 116, 117, 157
    test of, 123, 124
  limb, 116, 157
  partial, 117, 120
  rigid, 116
catharsis, 13, 168
Chevreul pendulum, 58, 59,
77
Chowchilla incident, 173
Christ, 37
concentration of the mind, 36,
39, 41, 56, 59, 76, 78,
80, 86, 88, 197, 205
conditional reflex, 147
conscience, 42, 44
conscious mind, 16, 42-47, 106,
140, 141, 155, 165, 171,
174, 201, 214-216
critical sensor, 141
crystal ball, 200

D

Davis-Husband Scale, 115-117
121, 149, 168, 195